# Twin Flames

*The Ultimate Guide to Attracting Your Twin Flame, Signs You Need to Know and the Different Stages, Includes a Comparison of Relationships with Soul Mates and Life Partners*

© Copyright 2021

The contents of this book may not be reproduced, duplicated or transmitted without direct written permission from the author.

Under no circumstances will any legal responsibility or blame be held against the publisher for any reparation, damages, or monetary loss due to the information herein, either directly or indirectly.

Legal Notice:

This book is copyright protected. This is only for personal use. You cannot amend, distribute, sell, use, quote or paraphrase any part or the content within this book without the consent of the author.

Disclaimer Notice:

Please note the information contained within this document is for educational and entertainment purposes only. Every attempt has been made to provide accurate, up to date and reliable complete information. No warranties of any kind are expressed or implied. Readers acknowledge that the author is not engaging in the rendering of legal, financial, medical or professional advice. The content of this book has been derived from various sources. Please consult a licensed professional before attempting any techniques outlined in this book.

By reading this document, the reader agrees that under no circumstances is the author responsible for any losses, direct or indirect, which are incurred as a result of the use of information contained within this document, including, but not limited to, errors, omissions, or inaccuracies.

# Contents

INTRODUCTION ..................................................................................................1
CHAPTER 1: WHAT ARE TWIN FLAMES?.................................................2
　THE HISTORY OF THE TWIN FLAME THEORY .......................................... 2
　THE ARCHETYPICAL EXAMPLE OF A TWIN FLAME RELATIONSHIP.................. 4
　ARE YOU ALREADY PART OF A TWIN FLAME RELATIONSHIP? ..................... 5
　WHY WE NEED TWIN FLAME RELATIONSHIPS ........................................ 6
CHAPTER 2: SOULMATES VS. TWIN FLAME .........................................12
　WHAT ARE SOULMATES? ...................................................................... 12
　THE 10 TYPES OF SOUL MATES ............................................................. 17
CHAPTER 3: TWIN FLAMES AS LIFE PARTNERS ................................21
　27 TRAITS TO LOOK FOR IN A LIFE PARTNER ......................................... 26
CHAPTER 4: STAGE 1: THE SEARCH........................................................32
　PERSONAL GROWTH AND HOW TO PREPARE YOURSELF FOR YOUR TWIN
　FLAME................................................................................................. 36
CHAPTER 5: STAGE 2: THE AWAKENING ..............................................42
　DO YOU USE RELATIONSHIPS TO FILL YOUR SPIRITUAL VOID? ................ 42
　TWIN FLAME AWAKENING EXPLAINED ................................................ 44
　10 SIGNS YOU ARE ABOUT TO MEET YOUR TWIN FLAME ....................... 45
CHAPTER 6: STAGE 3: THE MATURING (HONEYMOON) PHASE..........51
　WHEN YOU FIRST MEET A TWIN FLAME ................................................ 51
　HOW TO STRENGTHEN YOUR PHYSICAL CONNECTION............................ 55

Light Awakening Symptoms.................................................................. 55
Dark Awakening Symptoms.................................................................. 56
How to Get the Most from the Honeymoon Period........................ 58

## CHAPTER 7: STAGE 4: THE TESTING (CRISIS PHASE)................61
The Main Causes of Turmoil in the Crisis Phase ................................ 62
Why Does Distancing Occur Between People Who are So Connected?.................................................................................................... 62
How Non-Romantic Twin Flame Relationships Create Turmoil ...... 68

## CHAPTER 8: STAGE 5: THE CHASING OR RUNNING ...............72
How to Recognize if Your Twin Flame is a Runner........................... 73
The Mirroring Exercise: ........................................................................ 75
Defining of the Runner/Chaser Phase ................................................ 76
Should You End the Relationship Forever? ....................................... 81
What to Take Away from a Twin Flame Relationship...................... 82

## CHAPTER 9: STAGE 6: THE SURRENDERING ............................83
What to Expect When You Surrender ................................................ 85

## CHAPTER 10: STAGE 7: TWIN FLAME REUNION OR JOINING ............92
Signs That a Reunion is About to Happen........................................ 93
What Happens Once You Have Rejoined Your Twin?..................... 100

## CONCLUSION...............................................................................102

## HERE'S ANOTHER BOOK BY MARI SILVA THAT YOU \ MIGHT LIKE...................................................................................103

## REFERENCES ...............................................................................104

# Introduction

Have you ever felt a connection with someone so strong that it was like a bolt of lightning coursing through your body? Did you ever meet someone, and after only five minutes of talking to them, you felt like you had known them for a lifetime? We all form connections with the people around us every day. Some will be a glancing moment and forgotten in minutes, while others will stay with us forever. Are those people meant to play a significant role in your life, or should you forget them and move on?

We are constantly being told there is a person out there who is "the one," but is that true? Is it possible that out of the billions of people on the planet, there is only one person who will become our perfect partner? With twin flames, then yes, there is a special connection out there waiting for you. Soulmates, however, are different, and life partners... Well, that's another story!

Maybe you believe, maybe you don't. This book will give you the knowledge you need to identify why certain people affect you in various ways. If you have soul mates or twin flames, surely life is perfect from the first time you meet? If this was true, then life would be much easier, but even the most tumultuous relationship can benefit from some insight into the journey they are on.

# Chapter 1: What are Twin Flames?

If you have ever met someone who changed your life completely, they may have been your twin flame. When you form a high-level spiritual connection with someone, it can lead to love, friendship, or a combination of the two feelings. If you have a relationship with someone who is intense, life-enhancing, and spiritual, this could be a twin flame relationship that will endure any obstacles or circumstances.

To understand the concept better, go back to the origins of the twin flame theory. When you know the reasoning behind the doctrine, you understand more about the connection formed with your missing twin flame.

## The History of the Twin Flame Theory

When considering the origins of twin flame theory, you can go back as far as history records allow. Nearly all civilizations have examples of separation of souls, yet Plato, the Greek philosopher, presents the most distinctive explanation of how humanity became divided to form two parts of the same soul.

Plato lived in the Classical period of Ancient Greece and formed a school of thinking simply known as Platonist. He composed a dialogue known as the Symposium in which he explained how the actions of the gods affected humankind and why the actions were necessary.

Originally humans had four arms, four legs, and two sets of genitalia. Their head comprised two faces, and there were three genders of humans. The traditional male and female were two of the genders, while the third was a hermaphroditic being with both sets of genitalia. In the Symposium, Plato stated these original humans were essential sources of labor and energy for the gods and other dwellers of the Higher Dimensions but were quickly becoming powerful beings. They threatened the gods, and it is written that the eradication of humans was considered.

Realizing this would leave the gods with no form of subjects to do their will, Zeus came up with a solution to increase the workforce while diminishing their strength. He separated the original human forms into halves. Each human then became the form we recognize today with two arms and legs with just one face and one set of genitalia.

While the process doubled the number of humans, it also weakened their power. The gods had created a form of slave that knew no pleasure and lacked the will to live. Humans starved themselves and died off, leaving the gods with a conundrum to solve. Apollo devised a solution, and that was to sew the original humans together and then divide them with a common bond, so they had a sense of purpose and desire. He reconstructed the human form with a belly button that became the redeeming sign that our twin flame still existed somewhere in the world.

Each human then became reborn. They were refueled with a desire to seek their twin flame and form a reconstituted version of their original self. The gods recognized that desire and emancipation made humans function on a higher level, yet the reality of them finding their twin flame was remote. This suited their purpose because when humans find their mirror image, they become a powerful force that rivals the beings that govern them, the gods themselves!

# The Archetypical Example of a Twin Flame Relationship

Classical Greek history also gives us an example of the sacred lover archetype, Aphrodite, and Ares.

Ares is the divine male twin flame and the god of war. Aphrodite is his twin feminine flame and is also the goddess of love and beauty. They should have been repulsed by each other as they represent polar opposites with their beliefs and powers. Aphrodite was married to a powerful but ugly god called Hephaestus, who neglected his beautiful and frustrated wife by spending his nights in the workshop. Ares and Aphrodite took advantage of the situation and met to make love until dawn every evening.

It has been well reported that the Greek gods encouraged affairs with other people; they didn't encourage any form of fidelity. When the god Helios caught the lovers in a flagrant position, the story of their love enraged the gods, and they punished the lovers by separating them for eternity. These twin flames would not be kept apart by rules, and even following the godly declaration, they met regularly and produced seven children from their union! The god of Eros, whose powers include love, youthful magic, and sex, was one of these children and serves as a powerful reminder of what can happen when twin flames procreate.

Some people believe that it automatically means you will become romantically involved when you meet a twin flame. While this can be true, your twin flame could be a friend, a mentor, or even a student. They will often enter our lives when we are desperate for help. They form intense relationships that help us to steer through times of need. Twin flames will form relationships so intense it is uncommon for them to be lifelong relationships, so separation is sometimes inevitable.

It's okay for twin flame relationships to end, considering such levels of intensity can be unhealthy. When twin flames separate, it is painful, but the two people are left with crucial answers to life lessons and a feeling they have encountered their cosmic partner.

# Are You Already Part of a Twin Flame Relationship?

Do you have a yin to your yang? Do you have a relationship with someone who completes you?

Here are some of the most common signs you are already connected to a twin flame:

1) Time is irrelevant to both of you. You can spend hours with each other and never get restless or bored. You both wonder where the time has gone, yet you feel ready to do it all again the following day.

2) Déjà vu: During conversations, you discover strange coincidences in your present and former experiences. It seems like life is forming a path, so you both reach each other. You are destined to have a relationship.

3) You both feel a magnetic force that crackles when you meet. You feel a connection between your physical and spiritual energies, and you form an unspoken understanding.

4) Your strengths make a perfect foil for their weaknesses and vice versa. Together you are a force to be reckoned with and are virtually unbeatable.

5) You have a shared sense of purpose. The ideas you hold dearest are a shared value you both strive to achieve.

6) As twins, you know each other inside out, flaws and all, and never judge each other.

7) You will disagree because you are comfortable that you will always resolve your differences, no matter how often you fall out.

8) You are connected on many levels. You may be partners, friends, shoulders to cry on, or mentors to each other.

9) You have synchronicity in your former lives. Sometimes you discover uncanny parallels in your personal history; for instance, you may have both been in the same place during a historic event like 9/11 without realizing it.

10) You grow as a couple and become more sympathetic, forgiving, and empathetic to others.

## Why We Need Twin Flame Relationships

Contrary to some beliefs, we are a complete being even without this spiritual coupling. We all have a complete soul that can be strengthened by our own experiences, but a twin flame relationship helps you reach another level. These relationships help you shed all egos, understand what your hearts need to heal, and take the first steps to become a spiritually enhanced human.

The purpose behind your relationship with your twin flame can take many courses, but it will inevitably lead to a harmonious and balanced coupling with a positive outcome. This can include raising children, forming a bond especially important when it comes to ecological matters, doing business with each other, or becoming a spiritual mentor to each other.

Sometimes you can miss the signs that lead you to your twin flame. Outside influences may leave you feeling incapable of receiving the gift of a spiritual relationship and leave us unreceptive to the connection. You can be overwhelmed with emotions that leave you drained and flat, so you miss recognizing the signs you are in the presence of a twin flame. Maybe you are grieving or trapped in a bad relationship. When you may need spiritual help, the emotional points may be the reason you're failing to acknowledge their presence.

It doesn't matter if you seek a new spiritual connection or are simply meeting new people; it is essential to know how people make you feel. This can also apply to individuals we already live with or have in our life. They could be part of your spiritual makeup without you realizing the fact!

### 15 Things to Look for When You Meet a Potential Twin Flame

1) You always come away from spending time with them feeling like you've learned something. If you meet someone for the first time and feel like they can teach you something without you feeling inadequate or incompetent, then you may have encountered a twin flame. If you also feel like you have shared knowledge that could be world-changing, this could be your spiritual twin flame!

2) You immediately feel like this person is a safe place for you to go. When you meet someone who is completely trustworthy and will guard your secrets and thoughts, this can feel like coming home.

3) You know they will never judge you or reject you. This doesn't mean they won't be truthful with you or fail to pull you up when you mess up. They are so confident in your relationship they are probably the only person to tell you the whole truth with clarity that most people lack. They aren't afraid that you can't handle the truth, and they know how to work with you to become the better person you both know lies below the surface.

4) You never have to put a show on for them. If you feel awful, then you can act like it, and they will know exactly what to do. They will never berate you for having human emotions, but they will accompany you on the journey these emotions take you on.

5) You both have dark and light sides that complement each other. When your dark side is prevalent, they will display their light side to create a balanced, harmonious feeling. They instinctively know what mood you are in and how to be sympathetic to your aura.

6) You fall in love unconditionally. Every person loves another person or persons, such as parents and friends, past lovers or people who played an important part in their life, but falling in love is different. Twin flames fall in love despite convention and circumstances dictating it is wrong. They are unaffected by reality and any form of mental clarity. The heart wants this relationship, and it is a natural progression for both people.

7) You become scared of the relationship and want to bail. In the early stages of a twin flame relationship, you can feel overwhelmed by your emotions' intensity and depth. People can reach for their mental sneakers and withdraw. Imagine the coyote and roadrunner, and you get what this can look like. They are crazy, running around as one chases the other before quickly turning and becoming the one being pursued. We will discuss this aspect of twin flame relationships further into the book.

8) You don't feel threatened by spending time apart. You know that when you are together, you are bonded and form a single unit, but you still have your sense of freedom. Twin flame relationships shouldn't feel like they are smothering you; they should be strong enough to last, even when you aren't together. If you meet someone who is the embodiment of everything you want, yet you are never anxious about being apart, they could be your twin flame.

9) You are finely tuned to each other's energy. If you have a spiritual connection, you immediately know how the other person is feeling. You know with just a glance when they are happy, sad, angry, or upset, and you know they can feel the same level of empathy towards you.

10) You feel a sense of completion. If you have been waiting for someone your entire life, you will know immediately that your search is over. Everybody knows that journeys can be arduous, especially when they are undefined by time. That relentless searching for a feeling of togetherness will stop once you meet your twin flame. You will experience a feeling of arrival at your destination, and you will happily step off the path of discovery.

11) You will be a mirror for their fears and desires. For example, if you are a creative soul who can create art and beauty with any medium, then your twin flame will probably be repressed and more likely to have no interest in the creative arts. If you are a messy, disorganized soul, then your twin flame will be a neat freak who demands high levels of the organization. If you are a dramatic character who overreacts in stressful situations, he or she will be a strong and willful partner who knows how to talk you down.

12) Your relationship with your twin flame will highlight how shallow your other relationships have been. When you connect with your twin flame, you will feel a depth and intensity you have never felt before. This doesn't mean that former relationships are irrelevant; after all, every relationship we have should teach us something. It merely highlights that spiritual connections are far more intense than physical or familial relationships ever can be.

13) You can't think of a single thing you would change about them. There are no rose-colored glasses in a twin flame relationship, and you both understand how the other person ticks. The difference is you embrace the flaws along with the qualities you both bring to the table. You know that as a unit, you are spectacular, and you don't want to change a thing! You may both be at different spiritual stages, but your prime objective is to help each other reach a higher level and discover your purpose.

14) There is no sense of competition. If you have a twin flame relationship, you will have a healthy respect for each other. You will celebrate their successes just as they celebrate yours. There is no room for envy and resentment when it comes to life success levels. You may be more or less successful than your twin, but it is never a problem. You aren't competing; you are striving to become better as a couple.

15) They will be ready to commit fully to your relationship. This doesn't just apply to romantic relationships, as the word commitment can apply to all forms of unions. When a friend commits to another friend, it means they will be there for them no matter what. You know whom you can trust to have your back and who is just a friend of convenience. Friends should come in all forms of commitment levels; the trick is to recognize them. Your twin flame will cross rivers and mountains to come to your side whenever you need them, and they will stand by your side no matter what.

The key part to understanding what twin flames are and how they affect your life is to remember that forces bigger than all of us are in force. You may not be ready to connect, but it is still essential to understand the signs that show you when the opportunity presents itself. Your twin may be unreceptive because they aren't at a stage in their life to meet you. Hold tight because your time will come, and meanwhile, you will gain the experience of how to analyze the other people you have in your life and your relationships with them.

# Chapter 2: Soulmates vs. Twin Flame

What are the differences between these types of relationships? You already know something about what a twin flame brings to a relationship, so what do soulmates mean to you?

## What are Soulmates?

They are people who will enter your life and influence it deeply. They are aligned to your soul and may even have been a major part of your former life. Just like twin flames, they will mirror you to some extent, and when you look at them, you can see your own weaknesses and strengths. However, the difference between soul mates and twin flames is the depth of the connection.

You have only one twin flame who is the embodiment of the other half of your soul, while your soulmates are extensions of your spiritual being. You will meet many soulmates in your life, and they will come in different forms. They will come into your life to shake things up and make your life more meaningful. They may form romantic attachments, or they may be friends who make your life more enjoyable.

Sometimes, the term *soulmate* can put pressure on a relationship. If one person describes the other as a soulmate, it's daunting to live up to that expectation. True soulmates should have easier relationships than others and have a natural flow without dark or difficult aspects. They are intense but joyful compared to twin flame relationships, which will often be torrid and filled with extreme emotions. Your soulmate should make you feel close to them and comfortable in their company.

Soulmates may come into your life for long periods and be around as a rock for you, or they may be the catalyst that sparks an idea and then departs from your life in a matter of minutes. Soulmates have a give and take relationship, and they will sometimes push you outside of your comfort zone when needed. Soulmates are meant to teach us life lessons and improve our spiritual strength. They will help you raise your spiritual consciousness while twin flame relationships work together to raise the entire world's spiritual consciousness.

You will meet many soulmates during your time on earth, yet you may never meet a twin flame. That's not meant to be a statement that should make you feel sad. Your twin flame is a special part of your soul, but you don't have to connect with them to have a successful and fulfilled life. You are complete as you are, but if you are blessed with a twin flame connection, then you will work together to create intense energy that can be arduous and painful yet filled with the most intense love.

### The Signs You Have Met Someone From Your Soul Group

Your soul group comprises people with whom you have a natural connection. You will connect with them on a mental, emotional, physical, and spiritual level without knowing why. The energy between you will resonate so strongly it may feel physical. Soulmates create strong bonds that can transcend time and create vibrations that will create harmony within the group.

Soulmates within your soul group can be from different backgrounds, cultures, and gender and will often have diverse backgrounds that bear no relation to your own. What they do have in common is a strong sense of shared values and dreams. They believe in the same things you do, and they share the same principles and ethics as you.

You need to be open to meeting members of your soul group to benefit from the experience. They are all sent into your life to help you grow and move past fear, but if negative attitudes bog you down, you will not enjoy meeting members of your soul group. Many spiritual traditions believe that the obstacles we face in life are predetermined even before we are born. The people who enter your life as part of your soul group are chosen to help you overcome these obstacles and grow as a spiritual being.

### Where Do You Meet People from Your Soul Group?

This is one of the most important questions you can ask, and others will tell you to search everywhere. Although, if you chose to take that approach, it can take over your life. Your spiritual path is preordained, and the chance to meet your soul group will present itself when you are ready. That doesn't mean you should sit back and go about your normal routine changing nothing; after all, you can't win the lottery if you don't purchase a ticket! Once you feel your soul group's synchronicity pulling you in, you need to be ready to embrace the feelings and seek them out.

This process involves allowing your heart to rule your head and listening to your gut feelings. Your headspace will be filled with all your fears and safety measures that instinctively guide you on a safe and comfortable path. Your heart, meanwhile, is more inclined to take you out of your comfort zone and take a new path. Try following your intuition instead of your tried and tested methods of living. Embrace new experiences and the related opportunities they present.

When you want to meet new people and broaden your horizons, the Internet may seem like the last place to start. Online interaction is not something you would associate with finding your soulmate, but it is the perfect starting point. You can research new subjects, hobbies, and interests to discover your potential soulmates.

Create an online course for people in your area interested in the same things you are. A meetup course for cooking or art could mean you will meet like-minded people who may just be part of your soul group. Even if you don't find a soulmate immediately, you will establish new connections and increase your social group, which is always positive.

The local church can be a perfect way to meet people and become an active part of the community. Volunteer work is also hugely rewarding and gives you a sense of giving back to the community. It's true that as we get older, it is more difficult to make friends and form new relationships, so you need to put the effort in and say yes to new experiences. Stop checking out online contacts and liking photos from remote friends and concentrate on the people you encounter every day.

### How Do You Know When You Have Met Someone from Your Soul Group?

> **1) Your Eye Contact is Intense:** When you look into someone's eyes and feel a connection that is familiar and comfortable, then you may have met a soulmate. They have a coupling with your soul that can feel ancient and unbroken, and it will never feel uncomfortable.
>
> **2) They Will be Soul-Centric:** Members of your soul group won't be interested in your social statuses, such as how much money you have, your status at work, or other ego-centric parts of your life. They will be more interested in your spiritual footprint on the world. Expect conversations about

environmental issues and conscious living as you begin to share your common interests.

**3) You Will Feel a Magnetic Pull:** Even if your meeting is brief, you will be mesmerically drawn to them and their energy.

**4) You Share the Same Beliefs:** Members of your soul group will often amaze you with their synchronicity to your beliefs. They will be on the same page and will often mirror your words and thoughts.

**5) You Have a Timeless Relationship with Them:** From the minute you meet a soulmate, you are comfortable in their company. You don't have an initial awkwardness or reservation. You could have known this person for the whole of your life.

**6) They Appear at the Most Opportune Moment:** You may be unaware of your personal sense of attachment, but members of your soul group will instinctively know you are ready to meet them. There are numerous types of soul connections in your soul group, and they will appear to you when you need them the most.

**7) Time is Irrelevant:** You could spend hours with soul mates and never notice where the time went. It's like the clock that governs your thoughts and actions has temporarily stopped working. You are so immersed in your connection you feel that nothing else matters, and you refuse to be distracted by life!

**8) They Will Challenge You Without Condemnation:** Your soul group is there to make you grow as a person and as a spiritual being. They love to challenge you and push you towards circumstances that will test your life skills and emotions. They will never abandon you and will always know the correct level of support you need at any given time.

**9) Your Soul Will Feel Energized:** When you have an encounter with one of your soul groups, you will come away with a feeling of nourishment. It will feel as if your soul has just had the best meal ever and is full and contented.

**10) You Can be Yourself:** Your soul group is aware of your true personality. You will never need to be fake or pretend to feel things you don't. The authentic you can rise to the surface and breathe deeply around your soul mates, and they will never judge you.

## The 10 Types of Soul Mates

Your soul group comprises multiple types of mates, so it is important to realize who can be part of our spiritual consciousness and common humanity.

**1) Soul Partners:** These are the most common types of connections and are formed with people you agree to partner with. Most people associate this type of soul mate with marriage and raising a family, but there are many other types of partnerships to which we can commit. Forming a company with someone can lead to a connection that makes them part of your soul group, or it can be as simple as a beloved sibling who is your life partner. Nobody can travel through life alone, and our soul partners are here to remind us how intricately human lives are weaved together.

**2) Reincarnated Soul Mates:** When souls reconnect in this life, it can mean they have unresolved issues from their past lives. They can also signify that the souls have spent countless lifetimes together. Whatever the case, this type of connection is one of the most powerful in your soul group, but you need to take precautions with the relationship. Try to disregard any residual feelings you have from past lives and judge each other on the person you are in this life. You may need to heal rifts and then let them go so both your souls can heal.

**3) Romantic Soul Mates:** This can be the same as a soul partner, or it can be an opportunity to grow with the relationship. Everyone knows that romance is not the only ingredient in a successful relationship, and these connections are not always meant to be long lasting. Romantic soulmates help us grow as a person and take the rough with the smooth. They may cause you devastating wounds or challenge you with their behavior, but they are fulfilling a purpose. They are teaching you how to form successful relationships, even if it isn't with them.

**4) Companion Soul Mates:** Imagine a life in which all your relationships were romantic, or family-based. That would be hell, right? Who would you turn to when you need advice or support from someone removed from interpersonal relationships? Your companion soul mate or mates provide you with the support group you need to keep going on your earthly odyssey. If your life were written in a novel form, some people would describe soul companions as your spiritual sidekicks. They may be in your life for a couple of months or decades; it doesn't matter. They are the food and drink your soul needs, and they provide companionship for your spirit.

**5) Soul Families:** These are not your actual physical family, but they are just as important. People worldwide who show the same passion as you do for particular causes or activities can be part of your soul family. Spiritual groups actively working to bring love and peace to our planet may never meet each other, but they will feel connected because of the depth of their commitment to the cause.

**6) Kindred Spirits:** These connections can be formed by a commonality that leads to shared experiences. They aren't always soul mates, but they are important to you and your life. Maybe you both have similar life experiences that strengthen your bond. Young mothers struggling with their newborn babies will turn to kindred spirits in the same situation. People in the same profession may become part of your soul group because they understand the tensions and stress your career involves. It can be incredibly satisfying to spend time with a soul who just gets what you are about.

**7) Soul Contract:** This is not really a part of your soul group but rather a contract you make with yourself. You become another member of your soul group and promise yourself to do something monumental in this lifetime. You may make this connection with someone else or with yourself, just knowing the depth of commitment will help you when struggling to reach your objective is inspirational and soul lifting.

**8) Soul Teachers:** These members of your soul group are sent to educate you. They may be traditional relationships you form with educators who help you through school or college, or they may be more diverse. When you form a relationship with a person who can guide the path your life will take, it can be magical. College professors or counselors can be soul mates who aren't just educating you; they show you how important your advice and counsel can be for others further down the line. They are sharing the gift of knowledge and the importance of sharing it.

**9) Soul Crossings:** You may feel that the most important part of your soul group is the people who are there for you throughout your life and are constant companions. This can be true sometimes, but the fleeting meetings we have with soul mates can be just as important. The phrase "ships that pass in the night" is the perfect way to describe these encounters. You may feel an intense connection, but the time and place aren't right for long-term relationships. This could be someone you meet on holiday and form an immediate bond with, but you lose touch when you return home. Or a lover you meet who has been diagnosed with a terminal illness and passes away a month after you meet.

The point of these connections is to help you understand that time is irrelevant concerning connections of the soul. They are all essential and teach us something, even if they are brief.

**10) Karmic Soul Mates:** What do you think karma is? Is it a system of punishment and reward where the universe deals out karma depending on our actions? Karma is a natural energy governed by cause and effect, and the members of your soul group that are karmic soul mates will help you grow and evolve. They enter your life at key moments and facilitate you to change direction. They may be positive influencers who will help your soul evolve, or they may be negative forces who will help you recognize when life is taking you down the wrong path.

Our soul group provides the support and encouragement needed to get through life. Remember that your soul is always craving new experiences and looking to evolve. Recognizing the people who form part of your soul group will help you facilitate this evolution.

So, what is the difference between soul mates and twin flames? You have multiple soul mates and just one twin flame. The depth of intensity will be off the scale when you meet your twin flame, and it has been described as a "soul mate on crack!"

# Chapter 3: Twin Flames as Life Partners

When we consider archetypal love relationships and how people describe their partners, the term "life partner" is often used. It creates an image of two people who meet, fall in love, create a family, and then grow old together. Life partners are meant to be there for each other through thick and thin.

So, with this in mind, is it ideal to have a twin flame as a life partner? In most cases, the answer is a definite no. Twin flames are two parts of the same soul and turbulently connect with passionate and highly charged emotions involved. You can't choose your twin flame; you are joined on a spiritual level. If you are destined to meet, you will. Twin flames will often push you into a dark place and force you to rethink how you function as an individual.

Twin flames enter your life to make you a stronger individual and take you to your highest highs and your lowest lows. The blind passion you feel for them will not always be sexual, but you will love them with an unhealthy level of toxicity, and people around you will often warn you to get out of the relationship. When you connect with your twin flame, you will feel like an addict. You crave the connection you have, and it is more important to you than all your other relationships.

Soulmates are also a predestined kind of connection. You have shared experiences, possibly from past lives, and they are often guided into your life to serve a purpose. When you need a soulmate, they can appear in any type of relationship. They may stick around or be gone once they have fulfilled their purpose; relationships with soulmates are not always about longevity.

So, what is the difference between these two love relationships and life partners? All the relationships you have had before you meet your life partner are designed to help you recognize the qualities you need in your choice of a life partner. The spiritual wounds and heartbreak you have suffered in the past are all part of the process that leads you to your ideal life partner. This connection is not just about romantic relationships, and they can occur in different aspects of life.

The more you accept love into your life, then you will be ready to accept a plethora of life partners who will make you a more rounded individual with strong relationships to keep you grounded.

**Definitive Types of Life Partnerships You Should be Looking For:**

    **1) Partner:** A great way to start is with the most traditional form of a life partner, your significant other. It may be a boyfriend, girlfriend, husband, or wife. Your definition of a partner doesn't matter; the term life partner transcends gender, sexuality, or fluidity.

    We all seek love, protection, and the need for a safe relationship we can call on to retreat to when the world is proving to be a bit too challenging. A life partner will be there for you when you need them and step up to the plate when you need them. Traditionally this involves the male partner taking a "hero" role with their woman. They will step in and rescue their partner just like the heroic male they are biologically programmed to be, but the modern world has moved on, and women are more likely to play a different role than traditional heroes and damsels. They will expect to be just as protective as their male counterparts and be there for them whenever they are needed.

Does this mean that the hero instinct should be ignored? No, it shouldn't! It is built into male DNA, and they often need to feel some heroic role to keep the relationship healthy.

Here are a few simple ways females can keep their men feeling like heroes without seeming like a bimbo!

- **Make Sure They are Satisfied in the Bedroom:** Men are naturally programmed to keep their women happy in bed, so even if you aren't fully engaged because you are tired or not in the mood, don't make them feel inadequate. Act like you can't keep your hands off them, which is hopefully true, and tell them exactly what you love about them. Experiment between the sheets and have just as much fun planning new positions or places to try them. The best way to make men walk tall is to let them know they are keeping you happy in bed!

- **Ask for Assistance:** We all want to feel equal in our relationships, but certain tasks suit men physically. Choose the tasks that suit your strengths and ask him to help you with others. Let him open those tricky jars or help you carry stuff from the car. Why would anybody struggle with stuff when they have someone who will willingly do it for them?

- **Share Decisions:** Modern women are so often in control of their own lives that when they enter a relationship, they just naturally take over the decision-making process. This can be emasculating for men, but they will often choose a quiet life rather than assert themselves. Women must share major decisions like where to go on vacation or which place to book for dinner. Ask him for his opinion, and you will avoid any simmering resentment, and you may even be pleasantly surprised at his input!

**2) Mentor:** This role is typical of a different form of a life partner. They will be the rock you lean on when you need advice that is practical and from the heart. Some people mistakenly expect their romantic life partner to fill all the roles in their lives, and this pressures the relationship and can cause it to fall apart. This life partner can have played a significant part in your education, maybe a lecturer or teacher at school or college who has guided you to the path you are on.

It could be a person in the workplace who has taken you under their wing and shared their knowledge with you. Mentors come in all shapes and sizes, and some will be there for you throughout your life while others may bow out. Even those who have left are classed as life partners. They haven't left the relationship due to toxicity or disagreement and can be called upon for advice whenever needed.

**3) Anchor:** Whom do you turn to when your life hits a speed bump, or you need someone to turn to when your relationship is in turmoil? Your anchor is the person who will be there for you when you need help, no matter what the time or circumstance. You trust this person and have chosen them to be your life partner because of their intuitiveness and level of thinking. This is not a relationship where your anchor will agree with you on all levels and back you up; this is a relationship that will help you consider all sides. They will play the devil's advocate and suggest different ways to go for you in the future. Anchors will ground you and help you set achievable priorities in your life.

**4) Confidante:** This type of life partner is the one you tell your deepest, darkest secrets to. You know this relationship is unbreakable, and your secrets are safe with your confidante. You know you can talk to them in ways that others may find shocking. You can share how you really feel about the woman at work who everybody loves, and you don't understand why. Your confidante won't judge you or call you out for being nasty. They will probably have some equally cutting things to say about the people you know that will have you both in fits of laughter. Having a person with whom you can be as mean as you like helps you keep the rancor out of your "normal" life. We all need to let off steam now and then, and your confidante understands this.

The main difference between soul mates, twin flames, and life partners is all about the connection you form. Soul mates and twin flames will automatically know you; they understand what drives you and how your spiritual being functions. Life partners need to learn about you. You are forming a relationship with life partners without the same history as soul mates and twin flames.

You won't feel a deep level connection immediately; in fact, it may never occur, and that's not a bad thing. Deep spiritual relationships often come with baggage. There are intense emotions involved both in this life and previous ones, which can affect both partners. These connections are designed to test your boundaries and will often cause intense pain and heartache.

Life partners are people you have a lot in common with, and you feel a depth of love just as important but needs to grow. Spiritual connections are more like a jolt of energy that is unexplained and can rock you to the core of your being. Life partners generate a love like a plant; it needs to be fed and watered and will grow as time progresses. If treated correctly and nurtured, it will bloom and flower while providing you with strong roots, and you will see the fruits of your labor.

Perhaps the most significant thing to remember about a life partner is that you will have a choice. Twin flames and soul mates have a predestined part to play in your life, so balance it out with your life partners. They represent your personality and life choices and mirror the values and qualities you hold.

Remember that a twin flame and soul mate will often cause you pain, and that's okay. Yet, it is also the main reason you will need to break contact with them at some point. A life partner is someone you have spent your life with, and you trust they will not cause you pain, although some probably will.

## 27 Traits to Look for in a Life Partner

**1) A Strong Sense of Who They Are and What They Want:** You need someone complete. When you form a relationship with a life partner, they need to be in the right frame of mind to become committed. If your life partner needs you to define them, then you probably will spend all your time propping them up, and that's not healthy.

**2) Honesty:** We all tell white lies and know how to bend the truth with our partners. Should you tell them just how much you hate their new hairstyle or outfit? No, you use tact and diplomacy to save hurting their feelings, and that's part of being a decent partner. Lying is different. The minute your partner tells you a lie, you lose trust and respect.

**3) Delight:** You need to feel a sense of joy when you see this person. If you feel anything other than total pleasure in their company, then they shouldn't become part of your life partnership team.

**4) Morality:** Choose life partners that believe in the same moral code as you, and you won't be disappointed by your choice. Never compromise on the principles you both have. It's okay to have different beliefs and goals, but you should share the same level of integrity.

**5) Responsibility:** You need to choose people who are just as accountable for your life as they are for theirs. They need to be willing to invest in you and be there when you need them.

**6) A Shared Sense of Humor:** Everybody has different things that make them laugh, but you do need a life partner with whom you can share funny stuff. Make sure they don't take themselves too seriously and can laugh at life. You will need that shared humor when times get tough.

**7) Inner Strength:** When you are feeling weak or vulnerable, you need to know they have the strength to prop you up. This can be a strength physically present – as well as mental strength. Sometimes you just need to be the one being looked after and embrace it!

**8) Ability to Trust:** Some people are unwilling to lean on others and find it hard to trust other people. A balanced relationship means that both partners can be strong ones whenever the need arises. Your life partner needs to be in a position they can trust you to take the lead.

**9) Maturity:** You must be both at the same point of emotional development in a loving relationship. Mentors and anchors can be different, but you both need to be adults in a loving relationship. Immaturity is not an attractive quality in your life partner, and it will soon become a problem if your partner becomes an adolescent in your relationship.

**10) Compatibility:** This should be evident from the first day you meet. If you clash over simple things, then the chance of forming a successful life partner relationship is slim. You can't work on your reciprocity because it is a fundamental part of the relationship.

**11) Independence:** A successful relationship means that spending time apart isn't a problem. Life partners should have separate interests and hobbies and realize that independence should be a part of who you are. Never give up your identity to become part of a couple. Your identity should be what makes you so attractive to your life partner and a major reason they love spending time with you.

**12) The Same Level of Commitment:** Avoid people wary of commitment. A relationship will only grow when you are both on the same page. This doesn't mean you need to take things too quickly, but you need to know that a life partner won't bail on you once the level of commitment is raised.

**13) Vulnerability:** If someone has their emotional walls up, then you won't be able to form a fulfilling relationship with them. Humans are naturally vulnerable, and while it is essential to have barriers, you also need to know when to let them down. This applies to partners as well; how can you get close to someone who is impenetrable?

**14) Ability to Debate:** While life partners may not be as contentious as twin flames or soul mates, differences will inevitably occur. You need to know that your potential life partner can thrash things out so it suits you both. If they tend to sulk or shout without resolving problems, then you will both become frustrated when arguing.

**15) Humility:** While self-assurance is a quality that can be incredibly attractive, self-centeredness is less attractive. Humility is essential in a life partner; after all, if they are incapable of admitting their mistakes, you will be blamed for things for which you aren't responsible.

**16) Affection:** Some people are comfortable with public displays of emotion, while others are more discreet. Both attitudes are fine, but make sure your potential life partner has the same attitude as you do. If your life partner is keen to hold hands and kiss in public, but you aren't, it will lead to problems. Similarly, if you need affection and they are unwilling to give it, you will feel neglected.

**17) Empathy:** Life partners are there for you, so the ability to show empathy is essential. They may not fully understand what you are going through, but they should be able to comfort you and make you feel better.

**18) A Balanced Sense of Ambition:** When you form a loving life partnership, you need to be clear about what you expect from the relationship. For instance, if one of you is content to live in a comfy family home and work a regular 40-hour week to pay the bills and the other one wants to be the C.E.O. of his own company and is willing to work 18-hour days, then it can cause conflict. Some couples will make it work, but they need to know what lies in store for the future and any concessions they need to consider.

**19) A Healthy Attitude to Relationships:** This doesn't mean they have to show a perfect dating history; after all, relationships take many forms. They need to have a sense of family, whatever that means to them. It could be their relationship with their actual family or the bonds they have with co-workers. The main thing to watch out for is people who have no relationships; this isn't normal and can be a red flag regarding their ability to form new relationships.

**20) Open-Mindedness:** Nobody wants an inflexible partner. You need to know you will grow as a partnership and embrace new ideas and experiences.

**21) Faithfulness:** Without fidelity, a loving relationship will fail. Even if both parties commit to an "open" relationship, the cracks will appear quickly. You need to know that when your partner is somewhere else, they are still faithful to you.

**22) Mutual Sexual Attraction:** Loving life partnerships often thrive better with a healthy dose of lust thrown into the mix! You need to know that the attraction you feel is mutual, and you both want to rip each other's clothes off at any given time. You also understand that you will feel the same way even when your potential partner feels unattractive because of illness, for example.

**23) Curiosity:** A naturally inquisitive nature is part of a successful life partnership because you both know you won't tire of life any time soon. You want to choose someone who will be your willing partner in life's adventures and a perfect companion for the future.

**24) Flexibility:** You need to know that your potential life partner knows that life is full of opportunities, and sometimes they will need to drop what they are doing and roll with it! Life is a series of natural events and spontaneity. If you are too busy making plans, it will pass you by.

**25) Forgiveness:** Nobody is perfect, and you will make mistakes that will hurt each other. Your potential life partner needs to be a tolerant person who won't hold grudges and can forgive freely.

**26) Enjoy Simple Pleasures:** Life isn't filled with huge, monumental experiences; it is mostly mundane and uneventful. So, if your life partner is a positive soul who derives pleasure from everyday experiences and encounters, they will bring joy into your life. Sharing a piece of pizza or watching the sunset in the evening may not seem life-changing, but if they are enjoyed with your life partner, they can be unbeatable!

**27) Communication:** The cornerstone of all relationships. Your set of life partners should know how to reach you on every level. They should be articulate, knowledgeable, and great communicators because you need people who are eloquent and open to discourse.

# Chapter 4: Stage 1: The Search

When you search for something, it can become a mission like no other. You may be searching for your perfect home, which means you spend all your time online checking out listings, visiting districts, or aimlessly driving around looking for real estate signs outside of properties. You know what you want and how to look for it, but the search can become all you think about. When that happens, you can neglect other areas of your life.

Perhaps you have experienced this type of obsession and think this is the perfect way to search for your twin flame. Well, the news is in, and searching for your twin flame is a process unlike any other you will experience. You aren't looking for a physical object or something that is essential for your daily life. You are looking for a spiritual connection with a part of your soul separated from you for many millenniums, and the chances you will reconnect are slim. Does that mean you shouldn't try? After all, if the percentages of your meeting are so low, why bother, right?

Of course, people will take a negative stance regarding the search for their twin flame, but if you decide to go for it, then you are opening the possibilities of the most fulfilling relationship of your life. You could experience the ultimate form of spiritual fireworks and the most intense emotions imaginable. Does that sound like it's worth looking for? Then let's level the playing field and make sure you are prepared for the first stage of twin flame development.

First, you must understand the concept of divine timing, as this is the process that governs the twin flame journey. Unfortunately, the way we have been taught to think and view the world conflicts with the concept of divine timing. If you can change the way you think and adopt healthier thoughts about the journey to find your twin flame, then the process will become less distressing.

## Common Misconceptions About Divine Timing and How to Change Them

**Misconception #1:** You need to change yourself and your environment to allow divine timing to happen.

Consider how we view our normal physical world. What must we do to improve our situations and achievements? We must work harder and dedicate ourselves to the search for success. We must give 110% to everything we do, and only then can we expect to be rewarded for our efforts. We often think that our effort and dedication are the only way to achieve anything worth having. While this is true in the human world, the spiritual world is vastly different.

Cast off the 3-D concept and surrender yourself to the grace of divine timing. Allow the universe to dictate when things will happen and float on the flow of inevitability. Divine timing means you need to let go of the concept you control what happens next and just enjoy the gliding sensation of the current that is the universal flow.

### How to Fix Misconception #1

- **Surrender Your Ego:** Self-confidence is an important part of our makeup, and it can help you achieve great things that seem impossible. The spiritual world is different; you need to become part of something larger than your ego. Stop demanding that certain things suit your time frame or in the manner you find acceptable. Stuff will happen when the universe decides, and nothing you can do can change that.

• **Stop the Belief that You Have Any Power Over the Universe:** The physical world may be your domain, but a higher force governs the spiritual world. Your twin flame journey will take the path it has been allocated, and no matter how strong your willpower, nothing will change that fact.

• **Change How You See the Term "Surrender":** What does the term "surrendering" mean? Is it a sign of weakness or giving up, or is it all about laying down your weapons and understanding that certain things are out of your control? Try putting a positive spin on surrendering and change how you think about it. Allow yourself to be open to faith, hope, and a belief that a beautiful life awaits those who embrace this concept.

**Misconception #2:** Divine timing is based on the conditional version of behavioral efforts and will always result in rewards.

For instance, as children, we were taught that:

• If you tidy your room, you can go play with your friends.

• If you eat all your greens, you can have ice cream as dessert.

• If you behave well during the year, Santa will put you on the "nice list," and you will get plenty of presents.

• If you do your homework, you can play games after.

This is known as the "if leads to then" approach and, when applied to the twin flame concept, means we think we need to "fix" ourselves before we are ready to enter the physical union of our two halves. Although you need to be in the right frame of mind and open to the experience for it to happen, that doesn't mean you need to "work" on yourself. The most important work you need to do to ready yourself for the experience is dropping rather than fixing. This will be covered later in this chapter.

### How to Fix Misconception #2

- **Understand the Positivity of Divine Timing:** There are no punishment options in divine timing. You will always be supported on your journey, and the place you occupy on the journey is right even when it doesn't feel like it.

- **Have the Confidence That You Are Making Progress:** Your spiritual voyage is always advancing and will never backtrack. You may slow down and speed up as your spiritual evolvement blossoms, but you will never take steps backward.

- **Believe in the Universe:** Know that everything that happens on your spiritual path is happening *for you* and is benefitting you. Nothing is being done *to you* as a punitive measure. This concept is so different from the physical world; it's difficult to grasp. Think of it as life is your ultimate support system, and you will benefit from it for as long as you exist.

**Misconception #3:** Divine timing is a force that exists apart from our physical reality.

How do you believe we are governed on earth? Is there a vengeful force ready to smite us whenever we get it wrong? If you have been taught to follow popular religious ideals, then you are probably all too aware of the concept of a vengeful being that needs to be worshipped and obeyed. This leads to a belief you are powerless, and you need to please people and follow their doctrine.

Those who have been taught this, believe that the only way they can feel safe and accepted is when everybody around them is happy and content with their circumstances. This means everybody is seeking justifications for self-worth and looking to others to guide them on their journeys. You need to remember that you matter above all else and that divine timing is all about letting go of the "please others first" mentality.

### How to Fix Misconception #3

Now is the time to clear your preconceived notions of how you think about your earthbound self and its connection to your spiritual self. When you reincarnate on earth, a significant portion of your soul remains in the spiritual realm.

A larger, all-loving, all-seeing portion of us remains outside of earthly reality and works hand in hand with the universe or the ultimate source of energy to coordinate the divine timing that governs your spiritual journey.

Your earthly self is governed by human doubts and restrictions, but in the spiritual realm, there is a bigger, more powerful part of your soul to bat for you every minute of every day. This spiritual part of you is the ultimate cheerleader for your physical you and will work tirelessly with the original source of energy to align you and on how to meet your twin flame.

This extended part of yourself knows all about the bigger picture and will help guide you to the point of greatness where you are prepared for what the universe has in store for you. Put your trust in this extended part of your soul and let it take control. It makes things so much easier when you know the nudges it gives you, and you recognize when your spiritual self is making a difference.

## Personal Growth and How to Prepare Yourself for Your Twin Flame

Now you know how the spiritual world is geared up and ready to accompany you on your quest, it's time to get your physical self in the best form for the journey. This means you need to become the best version of yourself possible, both physically and mentally. You know that any future interaction with your twin flame will be demanding on your emotions and will create inner turmoil. This can affect your physical and spiritual health, so they both need to be at their best.

These suggestions are all about getting to know yourself inside and out. They encourage you to dive into personal development and embrace the process. This form of personal growth should never be considered a chore. Instead, it should be the ultimate way to get to know yourself from every angle.

**1) Create a Morning Routine:** When you wake up in the morning, you should be refreshed, filled with energy, and ready to face the world. Forming a routine means you are taking advantage of your elevated energy levels and making sure stuff gets done. Start with a healthy breakfast and a refreshing cup of herbal tea before you start your routine.

Try to include at least one self-care ritual like meditation or working out. Early morning routines are often the best time to clear out the clutter. So, start your day with positive actions by getting rid of some of the mess in your life. You will leave home feeling lighter and more organized.

**2) Absorb Information:** The modern world is a place filled with information. It can be overwhelming, but if you apply filters, you can learn something new every day. Information is power, and we all want to feel more powerful. You are growing spiritually, so take the time to grow as an individual. Read more books, join up for classes, or try a new sport. Even the least artistic people can create works of art. Painting, mosaics, pottery classes, or just doodling in a sketchbook all count as personal growth! Perhaps divine forces will inspire you to learn a new language because that is the mother tongue of your twin flame. Stranger things have happened!

**3) Work Out Often:** It doesn't matter what form your exercise takes; it just matters that you commit to it. Even 30 minutes a day is preferable to none! Get your body moving and release those precious endorphins that help your brain function more successfully. Not only will you feel better, it will also improve your sleep, your skin will feel healthier, and your body will feel the benefits almost immediately. Your self-confidence will be boosted, and you will just feel better overall!

**4) Talk to Your Spiritual Self:** You now know that much of your soul resides in the spiritual plane. Have a chat with this important part of yourself. Ask how it is and what it can teach you. Learn how to recognize the traditional ways the spiritual world connects with our earthly beings and what they are trying to tell you. The universe is not a subtle communicator! If you are open to communications, then you will get them! Any message they send will be loud and clear! For instance, if you are looking for a new job and appeal to your spiritual self for a hint, it will happen.

You may notice a stranger in your area who is appealing to you because of their style. You may love the car they drive or admire their style of dress. One day you will strike up a conversation with them when they mention a new company they work for who are currently hiring. In fact, they are hiring people for a position you would love. So, would you like the details and maybe a direct number you can phone? Of course, you would! This is an example of synchroneity and a clear sign the spiritual world is lending a hand.

**5) Write a Letter to Your Twin Flame:** While you recognize that a meeting isn't always going to happen, you are essentially connecting to them before you meet. Remember, they are the other half of your original soul, and you can ask whatever you like. How do you get to know people you are in a relationship with? You ask them questions and go on dates. So how do you get to know your twin flame or the other half of you?

You go on dates and ask questions. Since your twin flame is still a mystery, the best thing you can do is ask yourself the questions you would ask them. What are their/your ultimate goals? Who do they/you love most in this world? What type of experience brings them/you the most joy?

You get the idea. It may seem weird at first, but the process can be fun and revealing.

**6) Forgive Yourself:** This is a huge part of personal growth and can sometimes prove the most difficult. Hindsight is a beast for analyzing the past, and we can beat ourselves up over things that have happened, and we cannot change.

Here are a few common life mistakes you need to forgive yourself for:

- **Jobs You Didn't Take:** Most of us have made mistakes in our careers. Opportunities wasted or taking the wrong path are just a part of life. If you acted on your gut instinct when everything else suggested a different outcome, then you did the right thing. You will never know what would have happened if you had taken a different approach so let it go!

- **Money Matters:** If you find yourself in debt and struggling to cope with your finances, then do something about it instead of blaming yourself. Start with a frank conversation with your debtors and a practical plan to repay them. Being complacent and hiding your head in the sand will only lead to further regrets.

- **Friends You Have Hurt:** If you know that your actions have hurt somebody you care about, then try to make amends for your actions. Maybe it's too late for some people, so you need to walk away from the drama and commit to being a better friend in the future. Recognizing that you can improve is the first step to doing it!

• **Lost Love:** Relationships are a real kicker when it comes to regret. Many people find it difficult to get over relationships and move on to new ones. The road to new relationships should be free from obstacles and clear to travel. Remember, divine timing is guiding you, and it will help you realize when it's time to move on!

**7) Eliminate the Toxic Elements of Your Life:** Everywhere you look, you will find examples of how to declutter your life. All the so-called experts are telling you that if you have a clean closet, your life will automatically become better. While this is probably true, having a clean closet isn't really a major step for personal growth!

Applying the same principle to life is. Get rid of the things holding you back and stop being pushed backward by toxic relationships, habits, and environments.

Here are examples of toxic relationships you need to avoid:

• **The Controller:** Is there someone in your life who constantly tells you what to do? They tell you how to dress, where to go, and how to speak. Ditch them immediately and learn how to think for yourself.

• **The Downer:** Do you know someone who can find the negative aspects of even the most joyous event? Do they love misery and attempt to drain you of positivity? You know what to do! Get rid of them and surround yourself with positive energy instead.

• **The Perfectionist:** This can be a tricky one since we all need someone who encourages us to be a better person. Perfectionists will never be satisfied with your efforts and will fail to give you credit for any improvements. This will eventually lead to you feeling disheartened, so make sure you tell them their negative input isn't required anymore!

• **The Manipulator:** You know the type. They are masters at getting what they want while still making you feel bad about yourself. They know how to put an idea in your head that makes you do stuff you don't want and mess with your head. You don't want a game player; you want a game-changer!

• **The Competitor:** Healthy competition is great, and you should welcome it, but if you are in a relationship with an ultimate competitor who turns every situation into a battle, you will soon become drained of energy. You need people who will support you and be a team player, not someone who reduces your achievements to make themselves look better.

# Chapter 5: Stage 2: The Awakening

The next natural stage of the twin flame process is the awakening, also known as the yearning. Because the experience involves two halves of the same soul, their timelines may differ. You may have worked on your spiritual growth and be prepared to meet your twin flame, yet they may be unaware of the need to begin their search. This explains why this stage is described as a period of yearning when you may feel a spiritual void. You know a part of you is missing, and you may look for different ways to compensate for that missing link.

## Do You Use Relationships to Fill Your Spiritual Void?

As the song tells us, "All You Need Is Love," but are loving romantic relationships the best way to prepare for your twin flame? As you become more experienced in love matters, you may think that you will be better prepared for your twin flame connection. While you need to be in the best shape both physically and mentally for the meeting, nothing you experience beforehand can prepare you for the barrage of emotions you are about to undergo.

Immersing yourself in unsuitable relationships can make you less prepared to meet your twin flame. Be open to unconditional love and ready to experience the true sunshine of the spirit, and that won't happen if you are hampered by baggage from your previous relationships. It is human nature to seek a companion and benefit from the love and comfort they provide, but some people are too focused on "being in a relationship" rather than enjoying healthy relationships that occur naturally.

Do you feel the need to fill your spiritual void and lessen your yearning by being in a relationship? Here are some signs that indicate you may be using relationships to fill your void:

**1) You are Miserable When Single:** If you find yourself envying couples and feeling lost without a significant other, then you have a spiritual void. You need to be happy without being part of a couple. Try some following singular actions and embrace your singledom.

- **Travel Alone:** Go somewhere you have always wanted to visit. Choose somewhere you know you will love and create your own adventures!

- **Create Other Relationships:** Strengthen ties to your family and friends that may have weakened over time. We all grow apart from people, so maybe now is the time to reconnect.

- **Be Adventurous:** If you have ever held back certain parts of your personality because you were worried about how a partner would react, then embrace your weirdness and do stuff you have always wanted to. Karaoke in a local bar, roller-skating at the local skate park, driving a quad bike, or taking a course about cooking sushi are all fun options. It doesn't matter what it is, just do it!

**2) Your Mood Depends on Your Partner:** Empathy is part of a healthy relationship, but it can also be a dominating tool to control partners. If you feel uncomfortable being happy when your partner is sad, they could be in control of your mood. If you rely on them to feel joy, this is not healthy.

**3) You are Anxious When Separated:** If you feel negative emotions when you are away from your partner, you may need to work on your spiritual fitness. Every couple should have independence and enjoy their time apart.

**4) You Need Their Constant Validation:** If you constantly seek praise and compliments from your partner, this can be a sign you are seeking your spiritual value from them. You need to know your worth and be comfortable with your self-assessment.

**5) You Fall Apart When Relationships End:** It's sad when relationships end because you have lost something you once held dear. But if relationships didn't end, then how would new one's form? If you have ever felt completely lost or bereft when a relationship ends, or you feel your life has fallen apart, then it is time to fall in love again—with yourself! Step away from seeking new relationships and focus on your spiritual life and find wholeness of mind and spirit instead.

## Twin Flame Awakening Explained

One of the most frustrating parts of the twin flame process is that they don't automatically awake at the same time. This can mean that one part of the twin flame can be in stage 2 for years, waiting for their twin to evolve. If you know you are in a soul connection and are excited to meet your twin flame, you are probably the awakened twin flame while your counterpart is the sleeper twin flame.

This can lead to feelings of frustration for the awakened party as you fail to understand that they haven't felt such a strong connection and divine interaction yet. You know that you can connect to them using your higher self, and you feel their emotions in the same way, so why are they still un-awakened? This is known as the bubble love between the two souls when they can speak to each other and acknowledge each other's presence before they physically meet.

This can lead to interactions that may seem out of character. You may say something nasty or unkind to your twin via your higher self during this stage. You may be taken aback by these types of interactions and wonder why they occurred. You wouldn't say such negative things to your twin if you were face to face? Why did those thoughts and sentiments occur? Well, that's your higher self-helping you to push your twin's buttons and give them a nudge to wake up. This process is known as triggering, and although it originates from your physical being, it is an extension of your spiritual awareness. The order in which the two twins awake is generally dictated by the energy that drives them. The twin flame with feminine energy will generally be the first to wake, while the male energy is often awakened later.

# 10 Signs You are About to Meet Your Twin Flame

You may have spent years in the yearning state and spent the time interacting with your twin flame via your higher self. Some interactions will have been fractious, while some will have been joyful, but how do you know that a union is about to happen?

> **1) All Your Thoughts Are Filled with Love and Harmony:** There is no negativity and sadness. Your soul knows that it is about to meet its other half, and your lower vibrations will have been cleared. You know what is coming, and you are ready for the ultimate union.

**2) You are Happy and Shine with an Inner Glow:** When we meet someone special, it is often apparent to others by the light that shines from within. When you're close to a meeting with your twin flame, your spiritual self can't help but radiate its joy.

**3) Things in Your Life Will Change:** You may feel the urge to sell your home and move to another state, district, or even country. The feeling may be confusing and make no sense to you at the time, but this is the universe sending you a message. It is guiding you to a path that will lead to your twin flame. Go with it! Do whatever feels right and let your urges dictate your future.

**4) You Feel the Anticipation:** If you have constant butterflies in your stomach or your skin tingles with anticipation, this is a clear sign something is going to happen. If you know about the concept of twin flames, you will recognize what is happening, but people oblivious to the concept will feel a gut feeling of anticipation without knowing why. So, if it feels like being a kid at Christmas every day, then chances are your union is about to happen. Enjoy the sensation and ready yourself for the experience.

**5) All Aspects of Your Life Seem to Meet Your Expectations:** One sign of a forthcoming union is the opposite of change. Your life may reach a personal zenith to prepare you for your twin flame. Your financial and professional standards are met, and you feel more comfortable and happier than you ever felt before. That promotion you wanted, the car you drive, and the people who surround you are all positive aspects of your life, and you love them dearly.

**6) You Have Lost That Yearning Feeling:** This is a paradoxical sign you are ready to meet your twin flame. You stop obsessing about it and communicating through your higher self. You have never felt more complete and more harmonious. You need not feel complete because you are in the best shape of your life. You may even become dismissive of the union you used to crave because you wonder why you would need another person to make you whole.

**7) You Feel Inspired and Creative:** This is another sign from the universe that a meeting is about to happen. You will feel inspired to write more or start an artistic project. During your period of self-improvement, you may have already dabbled with new hobbies or passions, and the universe will use them to inspire you. When you become excited and passionate about projects and missions, you become linked to your humanity and more open to messages from the spiritual realm. Once these channels are open, you need to follow your heart and get involved with the projects you feel are your destiny. They make take you away from more lucrative projects, and you may wonder what the purpose is, but you must do them! The universe doesn't send you on fools' missions, and the outcome will be worth the effort!

**8) You Will be Able to Manifest Things for Yourself and Others:** Some people feel manifestation is difficult and think it is an unhealthy way to gain material things. A manifestation is simple as it is a positive way of thinking, and as you connect to your spiritual self, it's used to make people around you happy. You will feel a stronger connection with the universe as your union approaches, and the ability to manifest your choices will increase.

Try these simple steps to manifest things for yourself and others:

- **Establish Your Purpose:** Tell the universe what you want and how it will affect your world. So, a manifestation isn't about telling the universe that you've always wanted a Porsche, so could you have one, please? But of course, you are connected to your spiritual side, so you know how to use your connection to the universe to benefit other people as well. If you want a raise in salary at work, then you need to explain why you want it. You can then explain who else will benefit from your financial windfall and how you will use your extra cash to make the world a better place.

• **Plan to Help Your Manifestation Work:** Now, you need to create systems to facilitate an increase in your salary. Manifestation is just a part of attainment, and you need to give it all the help you can. Create exciting new projects at work and make sure the people in charge are aware of your input. Ask for an assessment from your managers or supervisors, and be prepared to ask for your raise if the outcome is favorable. Take courses that will make you more efficient and knowledgeable to make you a candidate for a salary increase. Help your manifestation in every way you can, and you will improve your chances of realizing it.

• **Allow Manifestations to Happen:** When practicing manifestation, doubts may occur. Remember that manifestation is subject to divine timing, just like the twin flame experience, and if it is meant to happen, it will. So, allow it to happen and stay committed to your goals.

**9) You Will Feel the Need to Raise Your Vibration:** As the time approaches when your twin flame appears in your life, you will naturally feel the need to improve your vibration and speed your personal growth.

This can include a desire to do the following things:

• **Improve Your Diet:** You will lose any bad habits regarding food. Your inner spirit knows how you should nourish your body and will direct you to healthier options. You will already have a relatively healthy diet, but you will feel repulsed by food bad for you as twindom approaches. So, if you are overly excited by vegetables and repulsed by your favorite fast food, then this could be a sign of your impending union.

• **You Begin to Avoid Electrical Devices That Emit Blue Light:** This is a sign you are becoming more aware of your sleep and that you're working to improve sleep patterns. Why do you want better sleep patterns? So, you can interact with your twin flame in your dreams and form a stronger relationship before you meet them.

• **You Will Feel the Desire to Walk Barefoot Whenever Possible:** You will feel a natural desire to shed your footwear and embrace the earth you walk on. If you find yourself in your garden with bare feet just feeling the sensation of the grass between your toes, then your spiritual self is preparing for greater things.

• **You Will Seek Alternative Ways to Heal Your Spirit:** If you feel an overwhelming need to expand your knowledge of alternative healing, then do so. Your body and soul are telling you that you need a level of healing before you meet your twin. You may feel an affinity with reiki healers or experts who practice acupuncture or crystal healing. Go with the flow and feel the benefit of whatever form of healing available.

**10) You Will Begin to Have Vivid Dreams About Your Twin:** These dreams will often be the most specific signs you receive. People who have met their twin flames have described their dreams before meeting them as realistic and intense. They share the experience of meeting their twin flame in their dreams and recognizing distinct features that prove to be correct. Twins will often use the astral realm to communicate while they sleep, but they will intensify the connections once they are awake.

During their dreams, they will often hug their twin flames and whisper words of comfort and reassurance. Some people have reported their twin would embrace them and say things like "I am on my way to find you" or "trust the universe to bring us together." Keep a dream journal and write the details down every morning following your experiences because they will help you recognize your twin physically and emotionally.

Details from these dreams will help you complete all the following stages that happen after you meet. The messages you receive need to be recorded, as they will be important to both of you as your relationship grows and matures.

The bottom line is that not everyone will experience all the signs above. Some people may find their meeting is out of the blue and received no warning signs at all. Other people will find that more physical signs are a precursor to their experiences. Numerology and specific patterns can indicate the imminent arrival of your twin, so watch out for them. The main thing to remember is to let go of any fear or trepidation and stay calm. Relax and enjoy the anticipation, you can't change what is about to happen to you, but you can improve the experience. Your twin flame is going through similar emotions, and they will be just as excited and nervous. Remember, when you do meet, you may be amazed at how much you already know about each other just from your spiritual connections.

# Chapter 6: Stage 3: The Maturing (Honeymoon) Phase

At last, all the signs showed that a meeting was imminent, and now they are here in your life and part of your very being. Your twin flame may have seemed like a far-off part of your life for so long you are finding it difficult to believe they're here. So, what happens now?

First, you must understand what qualities your twin flame brings to you and how they will change your life. The emotions you're feeling can be overcoming and often scary. They need to be recognized and appreciated so you can begin your twin flame mission.

## When You First Meet a Twin Flame

The signs we have met a twin flame are well documented in the chapter about twin flames, so we already know what to look for. Remember, it need not be a romantic connection; it can be a friend or a mentor. They will have the same struggles with life you do, and they will display the same strengths.

You will already feel a connection with them, and you may even recognize them from your dreams. They will feel the same intense connection and may be shocked by the sense of recognition. The intensity will be unlike anything you have both experienced before, and even a look can evoke the most intense emotions imaginable.

You both know you have been brought together for a higher purpose, and this can be overwhelming. How are you meant to deal with these intense emotions and the deep and meaningful love you feel and be productive? In these early stages, it can lead to drama, chaos, and confusion.

Twin flames are connected on a higher plane, but they need to exist on earth. This means they may need to learn how to temper their relationship and adapt to more conventional forms of relationship. Even if we wanted to "regular" relationships will still be required, and it is essential to integrate your twin flame into your life.

This means they need to know how their connections differ from regular relationships and how to manage them. There are four different elements to their relationship that need to be balanced and healthy.

### Discover Your Emotional Connection

The meeting of twin flames triggers the heart center's opening that allows them to love harder and deeper than ever before. Consider how a mother connects to their new baby by synchronizing their brainwaves to the baby's heartbeat, which facilitates an exchange of energy between them both. This means the mother is sensitive to the information their child is sending them, and they understand the needs and emotions their baby is experiencing.

In the same way, twin flames trigger hidden parts of each other that have been buried and unresolved in the past. Your twin flame highlights your shadow side and allows you to explore the aspects of your life that need forgiveness and understanding. Twin flames work as a team to give each other support and the courage to open their hearts and heal any wounds it may have suffered in the past.

## How to Strengthen Your Neural Connections

The spiritual bond you have will already be strong, but so will the fear that your relationship won't survive such a battering of intense emotions. This can lead to anticipatory anxiety. You may both be so worried about what negative things can happen that you fail to recognize the opportunity for positivity.

Twin flames already feel they mirror each other, but how can that sensation be strengthened? Much like more traditional partnerships, the honeymoon period is often a time for discovering what your other half is all about.

**1) Study Your Partner:** Your spiritual bonds may be unbreakable, but what are the more practical parts of your life you share? Remember, at some point, the two of you are destined to achieve greatness and the passions you share may be the key to discovering your destiny. Ask them about the joys and highlights of their life before you met and why they love what they do. What books do they love? What are their favorite foods and places to visit? You know you are special, but you still need to put the work into getting to know your partner.

**2) Develop Trust:** You must never lie to your partner and make sure you are always there for them. Be honest about your feelings, even when confusing and bewildering. Your twin flame should be the person you turn to in times of trouble, but they can also be the reason you are in turmoil! You need to communicate every emotion and trust them to be there for you.

**3) Fight Fair**: Even in this fairytale period, you will have issues with your partner, and it's tempting to use harsh words and accusations to get your point across. This can be damaging to both parties and can leave deep scars.

Try these simple rules when you disagree:

- **Know Exactly What You Are Arguing About:** Are you *really* having a full-on fight about dirty clothes on the bathroom floor, or is it just a handy reason to cause an argument? Sometimes partners will use petty excuses to cause trouble because they have underlying issues. Make sure your discussions are centered on real reasons and not just manufactured ones.

- **Avoid Absolutes:** It is much more dramatic to use phrases like "you never pick your clothes up" when the truth is saying, "I wish you would be tidier and pick up your dirty clothes," is more diplomatic. Avoid putting your partner in defensive mode and shutting down the argument.

- **Take Breaks:** If you are feeling emotionally battered, then ask for a time out. Acknowledge that the disagreement isn't resolved, and you know you still need to talk but give yourself a break. Take twenty minutes to walk off your intense emotions and return calmer and more reasonable. This can also give your partner time to regroup and see things clearer.

- **Honor Each Other's Boundaries:** Don't take cheap shots you know will leave a mark. You may feel victorious for about a second, but afterward, you will regret causing your twin flame pain. Above all others, you know the wounds they carry and the areas of their life that are sensitive, and how to land the most damaging blows. Be a better person and avoid cheap shots as they will only make your partner lose trust in you.

• **Extend the Olive Branch:** Know when you have both reached your limits and allow your partner to end the argument with dignity. Make a joke or reach out to hold their hand. All arguments should finish with a mutual recovery point. You've both said what was needed, so move on and recover the closeness you have.

## How to Strengthen Your Physical Connection

When you meet your twin flame, remarkable changes occur to your physical self and your spiritual being. The meeting of your twin souls will release a form of energy known as Kundalini. This energy will fill you both with such euphoria; you will feel the need to hug and kiss people while embracing life with a glorious feeling of energy. Though, it can also lead to physical symptoms that can be confusing to both parties.

Below we will consider spiritual and physical symptoms when light and dark forms are released. This doesn't mean that the energy is good or bad. It is simply a form of energy that exists within us and is released when we meet our twin flames.

## Light Awakening Symptoms

• You lose all sense of ego and feel a connected with the higher plane that is more intense than ever before.

• You feel blessed and bathed in love.

• You become at one with the world and feel intense compassion for humanity.

• You feel intense pleasure at the simplest things.

- There are no limits on your ambitions; you feel inspired to achieve greatness.
- You experience amazing synchronicity with those people you love.
- A veil is lifted on your past behaviors, and you understand the impact you have had on others.
- You can see how your mind works and picture the physical journey of your thoughts.
- The universe blesses you with "downloads" of information that allow you to become more enlightened.

## Dark Awakening Symptoms

- You can experience quite violent convulsions and alarming periods of shaking.
- You become extra sensitive to external stimuli, the TV sounds too loud, the lights are too bright, and you need to escape and be alone.
- You experience disturbed periods of sleep.
- You experience your self-identity transcending your body, and the lack of ego means it no longer affects your life.
- There can be periods of intense hallucinations when you struggle to distinguish what is real from what is imagined. This can lead to you feeling like you're going crazy.
- Feelings of impending doom that will dominate you for a short period until they are dispelled by the feeling of gentle energy that melts them away until they vanish.

These symptoms are quite common and can be terrifying, but they won't happen to everyone. Spiritual energy connections are individual experiences, but when you meet your twin flame, you have the added bonus of shared experiences to make you stronger.

Some people have reported that when they meet their mirror soul, they are immediately attracted to them sexually, while others report a loss in libido. This can indicate the sort of relationship you are destined to have with your twin flame. For instance, it wouldn't be appropriate to have a burning desire to rip your mentors' clothes off when you first meet them!

**Less Common Awakening Symptoms:**

- Exhaustion with no obvious cause can happen, and you may feel shattered and lack a spiritual center in the early stages.

- Dreams about serpents and snakes are sometimes present. Kundalini energy is often called the serpent energy.

- Feeling stripped of emotions and feelings defenseless like a newborn child is a symptom of your rebirth as a spiritual being and can feel terrifying.

- Highs and lows of energy levels with no obvious reason are other less common ones.

- Hallucinating sounds, and hearing music nobody else can hear can occur.

- You experience flashbacks to your former lives and recognize other people's past life experiences, especially if they affected yours.

- You are overwhelmed by sadness at the state of mankind, and you feel a need to repair the planet with your twin flame.

- You have out-of-body experiences when you transcend the earth and connect to your higher self.

- You experience food cravings and aversions just like a pregnant female does.

- You have intense orgasms even without physical contact.

- Undiagnosable physical symptoms like intense headaches, nausea, skin breakouts, and digestive issues can be symptoms of awakening.

This release of energy can be a joyous time for both of you, providing you are prepared for it. Be there to support each other and take care of yourself and your nervous system.

Become the compassionate crutch you both need and take care of each other. You are in the honeymoon phase, and this can sound like a perfect time, but it all depends on how you react to the barrage of new experiences you are undergoing.

# How to Get the Most from the Honeymoon Period

Just because you are twin flames, it doesn't mean you are somehow exempt from "normal" ways of honeymooning. This can be part of a romantic couple's timeline, or it could be two friends finding themselves on vacation. Taking a break from the relentless noise and stress of everyday life will help you both feel in a better place about your relationship. If you have a healthy budget, then the world is filled with dream destinations you can both explore, so let's consider some idyllic destinations where you can honeymoon in style.

### Spiritual Honeymoon Spots

**1) Omega Institute for Holistic Studies:** Nestled in the picturesque Hudson Valley, this retreat offers seasonal activities to appeal to everyone. In summer, you can travel to New York and join like-minded people doing a variety of events. You can canoe, swim or kayak on the lake or try walking the onsite labyrinth. There are classes in meditation, yoga, and other spiritual practices, or you can take advantage of the impressive 7,000-volume library to work on your creative journey. Visitors are encouraged to tailor their stay to suit their needs, and the staff will work with you to ensure your trip is everything you want and need.

**2) Miraval:** In the depths of southern Arizona, you can find this amazing top spa resort, ranked as one of the best in the U.S. While it may look like a traditional spa resort with all the luxury and comfort that entails, look closely at the packages they provide.

Miraval provides a unique experience called the Equine experience. They encourage visitors to let go of their fears and self-doubt by interacting with specially trained horses. They also have programs that deal with sexual aspects of life that can help you both work through any intimacy issues.

**3) Canyon Reach:** With resorts in four different parts of the U.S., the Canyon Ranch ethos is to help you achieve health and wellbeing. They offer balanced gourmet meals alongside nutritional classes to help you understand how food governs your overall health. They provide a medical check service to make sure guests have the right level of fitness to participate in their programs. This upscale retreat is the ultimate way to get fit and benefit from their professional services while still having the perfect honeymoon.

**4) Shreyas Yoga Retreat Bangalore:** This Indian ashram offers a spiritual paradise in one of the most beautiful parts of the continent for the more adventurous travelers. There are just twelve rooms set in 25 acres of garden, so every guest has a unique experience and is treated as part of the family. This resort differs from most spa-type holidays as it focuses on taking the guests on a spiritual journey. This includes more traditional yoga and spa treatments, but it is also about interacting with nature.

The guests are encouraged to participate in nature-based activities in the area and to visit local villages. They are given a chance to see how local children work in the surrounding fields, and they can help prepare meals at a local orphanage. This type of experience is guaranteed to promote soul searching and a degree of humility.

**5) Turtle Island Fiji:** This resort is more suited to romantic couples, but it can be booked as friends. There are never over 14 couples at the resort at any time, so you will never feel crowded or overwhelmed. Each couple has a private beach and can get married in a traditional Fijian ceremony that includes traditional attire and a wedding raft. Meals are served in a communal outdoor setting and served with the finest French champagne available. While this may seem rather luxurious and less spiritual, the setting is perfect for you to get to know your twin flame better.

Not everyone can abandon real life and travel to far-flung destinations to explore their relationships, so how are you meant to connect when other people keep interrupting? Share your favorite things. This can be as simple as renting a film (old style) and watching it with a pizza and wine.

Your mirror soul is just as excited as you are about the experience you are going through so take advantage of this. Snatch a weekend to go camping together and commune with nature together. Watching a sunset with the person you have been dreaming about for your whole life can be just as intense as visiting any retreat. Feeling the sensation of warm rain on your face can fill your soul with joy that is as satisfying as sex. Your connection is real, but it will also be subject to trauma, so remember to have fun as you enjoy the intensity of your mirror self.

# Chapter 7: Stage 4: The Testing (Crisis Phase)

When does the testing phase begin? This can differ depending on the relationship and the level of contact the twin flames have with each other. If you are living with your twin flame, then the testing phase probably will happen sooner. If you only see your twin flame at work or socially, then you may go for years before you reach this stage.

Most couples will begin to experience changes in their relationship following their first serious disagreement. We all know that even the healthiest relationship will suffer setbacks, but why are twin flames more affected by turmoil and problems in their relationship? The truth is because their relationship has ascended from a more regular 3D dimension to a higher plane, everything is elevated, and every emotion is heightened.

# The Main Causes of Turmoil in the Crisis Phase

Once doubts have set in it can open the floodgates for more negative emotions about your relationships. You have spent your honeymoon period believing you are bulletproof. Together you exist in a fairytale, and every day you notice new similarities between you and your twin. You have the perfect relationship, and nothing can break you...until it does!

# Why Does Distancing Occur Between People Who are So Connected?

Consider the facts. A "regular" relationship is between two people who feel attraction or kindred feelings between two individuals who can be quite different. Their personalities are contrasting, and their interests may be poles apart. They develop their relationship by trying different things and discovering if they can co-exist even though they are so atypical. That's the joy of regular relationships and finding out if other people can live with your quirks and foibles.

Twin flames are different. They are two halves of the same being, so they should never clash, right? Well, consider how you existed before you met your mirror image. Did you find every aspect of yourself perfect? Were you filled with self-confidence and never felt the need for self-improvement? Many people don't have those levels of self-worth, and this can be the root cause of turmoil in the relationship.

After all, it is a lot easier to love someone who is different from you and completes you as a couple. Still, if you don't love yourself as you are, then how can you love a mirror image of yourself?

If you are in an intimate relationship with your twin, then sex can be the trigger to your period of turmoil. The act of intimacy will trigger past wounds and traumas. You will both question if the accumulated negativity you bring to the relationship can be overcome. An overload of information can lead to a sense of drama, becoming the main focus of your connection.

### Why is Drama So Addictive?

The emotional triggers from both of your pasts can create a whirlwind of turmoil that means you cease to function in positive ways. You become too focused on the heartbreak and trauma from past experiences you are both stuck within the moment and will fail to find the energy to move forward.

Once the body experiences drama, the brain will release chemicals like those found in opiates. This means that as the drama escalates, the more the body craves it. Some people believe that love and attention only happen when they create a situation based on tension. They feel that testing the people who love them is the only way they will be sure they will stay no matter what happens.

Like other addictions, as the body and mind develop a tolerance, the level of drama needs to increase. For twin flames, this is even more apparent. They are the mirror halves of each other, and so, if one of them is addicted to drama, then they both are! As a couple, they will dredge up matters from the past to illustrate why they are so afraid of being hurt. They will be more focused on problems they can lose sight of the positive mission they should be focusing on.

### Here is How to Tell if You Are Stuck in Twin Flame Drama:

**1) You Are Always Telling the World About Your Relationship:** If you find yourself on social media changing your relationship status and posting on forums and blogs about your personal life, then you could be addicted to your own drama!

**2) Your Mind Replays Your Times of Conflict:** Even when you aren't with your twin, or you have given each other a break, you just can't let it go. Your mind is buzzing with the conversations and disagreements the two of you have had. This automatic analysis means you're constantly questioning yourself and your relationships with each other and other people. You will be overwhelmed by the fears and anger filling your head, and you will constantly worry about the past and the future.

**3) You Have Arguments with Yourself:** In your mind, you are persistently arguing with yourself about how the relationship is going. You play Devil's advocate for your twin and becoming angry with yourself and them.

**4) Your Former Identity Has Faded into the Past:** When you think about yourself, you do so as a unit. You identify as part of your twin flame rather than as an individual. Deep down, you know that your individuality is becoming a thing of the past, and it has gone missing since you met your flame.

**5) You Justify Your Negative Experiences and Compare Them with Other Twin Flame Stories:** If you search for examples of unhappy twin unions and comparing them to yours, then you may be focusing on the wrong part of your relationship!

**6) You Relentlessly Turn to Other People for Advice:** If you can't go more than a couple of days without checking the Internet for spiritual advice or consulting a tarot card reader, you may be in trouble. Insight into your situation should be based on your relationship and not on some "oracle" or psychic expert.

**7) Your Drama is the Main Subject of Conversation:** Have you noticed people rolling their eyes or making excuses to leave whenever you talk about your twin flame and the problems you are having? This is a sure sign you have let your relationship and the drama it creates take over your life. What about your other passions and interests?

## How to End the Circle of Drama and Focus on the Positive Aspects of Your Relationship

**1) Check Out for a Moment:** Step back, take yourself out of the situation, and catch your breath. Sit in a dark room and focus on your breathing while telling yourself that something needs to change. You know you are spiraling out of control, and it's time to get back to a form of normality.

**2) Clear Your Energy:** When you are in the crisis stage, you are filled with dark energy that governs your life. You're addicted to your drama, and it can feel like a track of music constantly playing on a loop inside your brain. Drama can get stuck in your psyche and follow you into your dreams. The best way to clear these feelings is to remove any negative energy and start with a clean slate.

Try these effective yet simple energy-cleansing methods.

- **Cut the Cord:** Who is the main protagonist when it comes to your drama? Your twin is, of course. But who else is on the edge of your relationship putting their nose into your business? Picture all the people causing you turmoil, and mentally let them go. Think of them and visualize a cord that attaches them to you. Now say, "I bless you with positive energy, and I let you go" as you cut the cord. Watch as they drift away and feel the space this leaves in your spiritual space. Each night as you go to sleep, consider what attachments you have formed that day and let them go.

This helps you sleep better with a clear mind and a healthy mental attitude.

• **Clear Negative Thoughts:** Take a notebook and write down any negativity you have encountered recently. When twin flames found a union, they can trigger some pretty devastating past emotions. These can result from decades of repressed feelings and can overwhelm your state of balance. Some of these thought-forms originate from personal experiences, or they can be as random as the opinion and expectation of others. Maybe you think you aren't good enough for your twin, or they deserve better. This is a harmful way to think, and you need to dispel any negative, redundant, and repetitive thought forms to make way for positive thoughts. Picture a bright white cleansing light to help eliminate any spiritual debris invading your energy field.

• **Create a Sacred Space:** If the emotional battles between yourself and your twin are inevitable, then you need a place to recharge. Your energy is like a battery, and recharging is essential. This type of space can be a physical space like a quiet room in your house or the local park. A trip to the beach or other local beauty spots will help you regroup and raise your positivity. If physical options aren't available, then create an energizing space in your mind. Picture yourself in space or on another planet to get the most from your visualization.

• **Have a Good Cry:** Have you ever wondered why children cry so often? They recognize that crying is an emotional release that also cleanses their energy and causes positive vibrations. As adults, we are conditioned to keep our crying to a minimum and put on a brave face when faced with trauma. Let it out. If you feel emotionally drained, you need to clean your aura, and crying will do that. You may feel unable to let go of your repression and seek a trigger to start you crying. So, put a suitably sad film on your iPad and grab a handful of tissues and let it all out!

• **Take a Salt Bath:** To clean your energy and your body, then this traditional type of relaxation is perfect. Salt is one of the most natural cleansing elements, and sea salt is even more effective. Use Himalayan, Epsom, or regular sea salt in a hot bath to draw out all the negative energy you are holding on to.

**3) Let Go of Attachments to Groups or Online Connections That Involve Twin Flames:** Your experience with your twin should be between the two of you. Yes, it's informative to channel into other people's experiences and get embroiled in their trauma and conflicts, but it can also mess with your mind. You can create strife without knowing it just by bringing other people's drama into your relationship. Detach yourself from outside influences, and you will have the chance to identify what is within your union that is causing conflict.

**4) Forgive and Forget:** Once your energy is cleansed, then it's time to build some bridges. Contact your twin and ask them to forgive you because you forgive them. This can help you start again and build into the couple you know you can be. You both need to be in a good place for this to happen, or you will end up back on the hamster wheel of emotions you are looking to get off. Remember that essentially, you are truly one and the same. Any drama and turmoil won't benefit either of you. In fact, it damages both of you and it needs to be addressed. If you feel your twin has deliberately hurt, you then consider what that says about their emotional state. Nobody hurts other people when they are in a place of joy. Hurt comes from hurt and possible fear of what is happening to you both.

**5) Replace Your Addiction to Drama with Another Positive Activity:** Even when you are determined to expel drama from your relationship, you must realize that you are both going to miss it and the part it played in your union. Fill this void with another healthy activity, so you can both move forward with a new pattern to replace the old one. Consider the part that chewing gum can play for people who are trying to give up smoking. Many former smokers will tell you that gum is more effective than anything else when trying to kick the habit because it gets rid of a negative habit by replacing it with a new one. Exercise, cooking, reading a book, or catching up with Netflix will all work. Eating a piece of fruit or listening to new music will also provide you with something else to "chew" on.

**6) Repeat When Necessary:** The methods explained above are not a one size fits all solution for twin flame relationships, but they will help. You may need to practice them every day, but only the two of you will know your relationship's true status. All connections require work to endure over time, and you have spent so long anticipating your romantic twin flame arriving that it would be tragic to let drama spoil it.

## How Non-Romantic Twin Flame Relationships Create Turmoil

Surely, when you connect with your twin flame in a way that doesn't involve intimacy or sex, you remove all the tension that romantic ties create, don't you? That is what we would like to believe, but anybody who has experienced the relationship between soul mates and ultimately twin flames knows otherwise.

Once you have connected to your soul group or your mirror soul, you have experienced a dimensional shift that transcends most human experiences. You are likely a spiritually healthy being to experience these types of connections, which can make you dismissive of other people who aren't as developed as you are. Even when you are becoming the better spiritual version of yourself, you are raising the bar. You are physically better and emotionally stronger, and you find it difficult to understand how other people aren't putting in the same effort.

This shift of perception can throw your world into chaos even before you meet your twin flame so imagine how the pair of you will react. Knowing what may happen to your individual and joint relationships will help you to prepare yourself for the inevitable conflict that will occur.

**1) You Will Lose Friends:** You are changing as a person, and the energy your twin flame connection brings will elevate you into a higher place. This will disconnect you from people who were in your life before you ascended, and they may feel uncomfortable in your presence. Your vibrational frequencies will clash, and they will feel cut off and abandoned. Some of the most influential people in your life, even those you have known from childhood, will fall away, but don't worry because you are now part of a different club. Tap into the worldwide twin flame experience and mix with people who understand the concept of twin flame experiences.

**2) You Will Change Jobs:** The shift of dimensions will affect all aspects of your life. Fact. You will begin to expect better things whenever and wherever you are. Consider it your V.I.P. status shift when you move from coach to first class. Your soul will want more, and it will push you out of your comfort zone to achieve what it believes is your destiny. You may blame your twin flame for these uncomfortable feelings and wishing you had never met them. This is just a phase on the road to your joint mission to success. There will be periods of unrest but hang in there because the outcome will justify the difficult times.

**3) You May Lose Contact with Family Members:** When your twin flame is not part of your more traditional circle, then it can cause conflict. Your family expects you to be focused on them and their needs and wants, so it can be disruptive when that focus shifts. As you change and expect better things, they can remain stagnant and uninvolved in your present activities, and that's fine. Families are all about drama and intrigue, so it can be inevitable that problems occur. Cut out toxic connections and concentrate on your spiritual health. Remember, just because you were born into a group of people doesn't mean you are tied to them for life.

**4) You Will Become Intolerant of Petty Actions:** You and your twin are filled with higher vibrations that let you live your true life without focusing on lower-level activities. The problem is that mere humans tend to indulge in these lower-level behaviors, and it will become repugnant to you. Gossips, bullies, liars, cheats, and fearmongers will all be discarded. The old you may have allowed for their behavior, but the newly enlightened you will lead a better life. You won't necessarily look down on them or pity their existence; you will just choose not to engage with them. Your twin flame may be blamed for your new attitude, and this may cause conflict.

**5) Alcohol and Other Stimulants Are No Longer Part of Your Life:** Once you have experienced the highs of twin flame connectivity, then there is no substitute. You understand what drives you, and it isn't the standard toxins on which other humans rely. Higher vibrational frequencies lead to a spontaneous natural cleaning of the system. You will become more affected by natural stimulants and, as such, won't need to turn to caffeine or sugar to raise your energy levels. This can lead to conflict amongst your social group since you no longer need to visit bars or coffee shops, and you prefer to feed your soul with trips to museums and culturally enriching venues.

**6) You Will Follow Your Soul Rather Than Your Ego:** You will understand the importance of the divine plan and how it governs your life. Once you let go of the traditional belief that your ego is running the show, you become more instantaneous and willing to go with the flow. This can cause conflict if your divine plan goes against other people's needs and wants in your life.

It's important to understand is that all twin flame relationships go through the conflict stage. Some will survive and go on to thrive; others will take a different path.

# Chapter 8: Stage 5: The Chasing or Running

At this stage of the relationship, you may both be exhausted by all the turmoil and turbulence you have been through. All those years of yearning for "the one" and wishing you could feel complete seem to be firmly in the past. Those heady days of attraction and love have been obliterated by the stress and anxiety caused by your crisis stage.

Chances are your souls are at different levels of maturity, and one of you will find the intensity more difficult to handle. The younger soul will often feel the need to escape, while the older soul will become the partner called *the chaser*. Most twin flame couples will experience this stage, but their length will vary greatly depending on personalities and circumstances.

If you become the chaser in your relationship, it's important to understand what to look for as your partner begins to run. Knowing the signs can prepare you for their departure and help you understand why the relationship needs to take a break. There should be no recriminations about separating; it could be the healthiest thing you can do as a couple, but the role you both play should be determined before you begin this stage of the twin flame journey.

# How to Recognize if Your Twin Flame is a Runner

First, you need to understand that the grand prize in a twin flame relationship is not always a lifelong romantic involvement. The male divine soul will often feel the need to have other relationships, despite connecting with their female divine soul. That's just how the masculine soul works, and there is no use trying to understand why this happens.

Runners don't always know why they leave; they just feel that separation from their twin is the only way to progress. This doesn't mean the feelings they have are less intense than the chaser, they are just less equipped to deal with them. The process will begin when the runner begins to doubt the connection is what they want, and they will begin to pull away in different ways.

**1) Ghosting:** This is possibly one of the cruelest ways of withdrawing from a relationship. It means the runner will suddenly, without warning, withdraw all forms of communication and fail to respond to any of your messages. Your first reaction will be to wonder what has happened, maybe they have been hurt or a family emergency has caused them to leave town. Upon closer inspection, you realize that they have cut you out of their life. You are blocked on social media; they have changed their number, and you have no other way of communicating with them.

Why would anybody choose such a brutal way to end things? If you consider it from the runner's perspective, it is a quick and easy way out. There is no drama, hysterics, difficult conversations, or explanations needed. They simply leave, and you are left to deal with the mess.

**2) They Bench You:** This is a method used by twins who are eager to keep all their options open. They will give you the love you need one day and then treat you like a random acquaintance the next day. They aren't willing to completely close the door, but they still want to see what else is out there. This doesn't always mean withdrawing sexual contact, as this is more of a 3-dimensional reaction to benching. With twin flames, the relationship will often transcend sex, and the runner will blow hot and cold about deeper relationship aspects. They will tell you their most intimate feelings and then treat you like a stranger.

**3) They Get Involved with Groups of People Who are Not in Your Social Circle:** When your twin spends more time with their friends or colleagues, they are trying to exclude you from their life. Don't be insulted, but be prepared that they may be leaving the relationship.

**4) Withdraw Commitment Levels:** Because of the nature of your relationship, there may be social taboos that cause society to frown on your union. While you may feel you can both get past these obstacles, they may be less convinced.

Here are some of the most common obstacles to twin flame relationships:

- **Age Gaps:** Your twin flame may be a lot younger than you, and your relationship could raise eyebrows.

- **Unethical Relationships:** If your twin is held back by convention, they may feel the need to run. Some examples are a lawyer/client, student/teacher, doctor/patient, etc. You may be willing to make the changes needed for the relationship to work, but they aren't.

- **Different Sexual Orientation:** One of you may be naturally gay while the other is heterosexual.

- **Current Relationships:** When you form your relationship, you may already be in loving partnerships with other people. Some twins will find it hard to abandon these partnerships and choose to be loyal rather than follow their hearts.

- **Distance:** Although your divine plan will give you nudges to take you to your twin, you may end up living on different continents! It may be easier for your twin to adapt to their physical surroundings rather than move and uproot their lives.

- **Cultural Differences:** Culture hugely influences some people, and your twin may feel uncomfortable shedding the beliefs and behaviors they have been brought up with.

### How Can You Repair Your Relationship?

Within your union, you are aware that you need help to resolve your issues. Your partner has upset you, and you have upset them. The type of love you both feel for each other affects you and is overwhelming. The following exercise is an effective way to place your cards on the table and have a full and frank discussion with your partner and yourself.

## The Mirroring Exercise:

1) Make time to sit in a quiet place with a piece of paper and a pen.

2) Now is the chance for you to put your issues down in black and white. Use short sentences to record your thoughts and emotions. Use sentences like "I am upset with my twin flame because he uses harsh words to get a reaction from me"

or "I dislike my twin flame when he pressures me to spend time with him."

3) Now, rewrite the statements with different pronouns to make them about yourself. For instance, "I am upset with myself because I use harsh words to get a reaction from my twin."

4) Are there any truths in the sentences you have just written? Sometimes the issues we have with others originate with ourselves. Are you misinterpreting things because you know you have negative reactions to certain situations? Are you pressuring your partner because you need to pressure yourself?

5) Imagine your inner pain and hurt as a separate physical part of you and have a conversation with it. Ask it what it needs to feel better and heal. Hug it and spend time with it until it feels healed. Only then can you let it reintegrate with yourself and become whole once more.

This exercise will help you have more controlled conversations with your twin and listen to what they are trying to tell you. Mirroring is a potent way to talk to your inner turmoil and should be practiced whenever needed.

## Defining of the Runner/Chaser Phase

When one half of the couple becomes scared of the connection, physical distancing doesn't always reflect it. They may lack the courage to leave the relationship, but they will become more distant.

Signs your twin is the runner even though they are physically staying put.

- **They Turn to Distractions Like Drugs and Other Stimulants:** Most people in twin flame relationships need not rely on external stimuli. Clean energy brings them all the pleasure they need, so when one twin turns to artificial forms of pleasure, they are looking to break free. Alcohol and drugs are the most common ways to find a release from the intensity they are feeling. They will do anything to block out the barrage of emotions that your partnership is subject to.

- **They Find Excuses Not to be Alone with You:** Do you find you are both spending less time alone? Does your partner surround the two of you with other people and grow anxious if the number of people dwindles? This can mean they need a break from the intensity that happens when there are no distractions. Let them organize your social life this way if you are comfortable with it. This may be all they need to convince them to stay. If you challenge them, it can make them bolt.

- **They are Overwhelmed When They are with You:** Less mature souls can feel anxious and stressed when faced with their mirror soul. They will display irritability when alone with their partner and try to cause disagreements as an excuse to leave. Mood swings are inevitable as they don't understand why they are experiencing such high levels of stress; after all, isn't this relationship the pinnacle of all unions?

Unlike regular relationships, your twin flame won't signal their unhappiness with physical or mental abuse. There is no excuse for this behavior in any partnership. Your twin flame shouldn't cheat on you either; they know the true depth of your love and would never hurt you or cheat. If you do experience this behavior, it probably isn't your twin flame.

Remember, the running phase is probably triggered by their lack of spiritual maturity. They may not have been fully prepared for your union, and they need to work on themself before you can form a successful partnership. If so, the best thing you can do for them is to give them your blessing and tell them you will always be there for them if they want to return.

## Will Your Twin Flame Return?

Here's the kicker: Twin flames that run away will often come back, sometimes more than once. You may be entering a phase of your union filled with separations and reunions. No one knows what will happen, but they will return if they are your true twin flame. The term *chaser* can be misleading. After all, you shouldn't physically chase them because *they decide when* to return.

## Consider Why They Ran Away

When one person is left behind in a relationship, it can be lonely, but it can also be rewarding if you use the time wisely. Take the time to consider these points:

- Are you sure they are your true twin flame and not just part of your soul group?

- Do you feel you still have things you need to accomplish together? Or do you feel that your relationship has reached a natural end?

- You may have unprepared for the meeting, and you need to do more work on your personal growth.

- You are not destined to spend the rest of your life chasing them; the decision is yours to make.

## How to Chase a Runner

First, don't panic. Relax and form a plan. You still have your life to lead and other relationships to maintain. It is unhealthy to put all your energies into one channel, and you still need to look after yourself, and your spiritual health. So, stop worrying about what might happen and concentrate on the here and now. Your twin flame relationship differs from anything you have experienced on the spiritual plane, so you have no point of reference. Avoid looking at other people's experiences, and instead, choose the best way to convince your partner to return.

You might be the more spiritually mature one in your twin flame connection, but that doesn't mean you need not work on yourself.

**1) Raise Your Personal Vibrations**: Remember when you were in the yearning stage? You knew a meeting was possible, and you wanted to be in the best spiritual shape when it happened. Have you neglected your vibrations during your time together? Have you been too focused on your twin to give yourself some love? Take the time to raise your vibration and let your twin flame know you are still there for them, no matter how far away they are.

Tips on how to raise your vibration and send love to your twin flame:

- **Be Grateful for the Time You Had Together:** It's impossible to feel anger and fear when filled with gratitude. Every time you feel low energy threatening to overwhelm, try remembering what you are grateful for. This is a great way to ramp up your vibes!

- **Visualize the Love You Feel for Them:** Imagine they are with you, and you are sharing the connection you have formed. Love is one of the highest vibrating states of being, and your twin can pick up your vibrations wherever they are.

- **Be Generous:** Are you feeling lonely without your twin? Smile at a stranger. If you are generous with the love you give, you will receive the same love, if not more, in return. When you give your time, money, and love freely, you raise your spiritual vibe.

- **Forgive:** Are you feeling resentful toward your twin? Do you blame them for leaving you alone? Consider their feelings. Would you come back to a partner who feels hostile toward you? Forgive them for all that has happened, and you increase the chances of them returning.

- **Choose High Vibe Entertainment:** Everyone knows the benefit of high fiber food and high-energy ingredients, but you are affected by everything you consume. Do your entertainment choices leave you uplifted or depleted? Fill your time with content that makes you happy and energized rather than sad and anxious. Are all your social media sources healthy, or do some leave you feeling insecure? Consider changing your settings to increase your vibrations by limiting your time online and communing with nature instead. Change your music choices and discover new genres you may love.

- **Make Sure Your Relationship Vibes are Buzzing:** If you have been too busy focusing on your twin, some of your other connections may have suffered. Get back in touch with people and surround yourself with people who make you feel good. It can be too easy to sit around moping the loss of your twin and to lower your frequency, but how will that help you guide them back to you? When you have healthy relationships with others, you are signaling you are ready to try again.

2) **Remain Open to the Signs:** Remember back in the yearning stage when you were aware of the twin flame's signs? When you are the chaser, the universe will once more step in and guide you toward reunion if it feels you are ready. If you see repeated adverts to visit a resort or another country that seem to fit perfectly with your timeline, then do it. Pay attention to the messages the universe is sending you, and you may find yourself in the right place at the right time! Of

course, the universe could just be telling you that you need a break following your recent turmoil!

**3) Talk to Them Through the Higher Plane**: You may have found it challenging to communicate your true feelings when you were together physically. Your own emotions and perspectives may have muddied the waters for communicating clearly. Now you are physically separated, it is easier to consider their side of any conflicts. They may be the mirror part of your soul, but you are both influenced by the experiences that happened before you met. You're different genetically and can have different personalities depending on the environment you were brought up in. Empathize with them and have conversations rather than arguments.

# Should You End the Relationship Forever?

If your relationship has been the best experience ever despite the contradictions, conflict, and turmoil you endured, then, of course, you want to reunite. Yet, most twin flame relationships are destined to be temporary as the work needed to maintain them can be exhausting. If you can ride the waves of emotions and reach a tranquil shore, then you might both stay together forever, but sometimes it must end.

Here are signs that it is time to stop running or chasing:

1) You stop regarding your relationship as a safe place to be. You stop thinking of your twin as your "home" as the trauma of your union has taken over.

2) You are cold and dismissive of each other. If you contact your twin and they are rude and disdainful to you, it could be time to call it a day. When chasing your twin, they should still treat you with respect, if not love. Twin flames aren't meant to be enemies. Ever.

3) You feel that chasing or running is a waste of time. If you lose interest in any part of the process, then the relationship has run its course. Have the conversation and end it properly. Your twin needs to know exactly where they stand as they may have expectations for the future. You love each other even if you can't maintain a partnership. Do the right thing and end it cleanly.

4) Your gut tells you to end it. It is as simple as that. You have trusted your instinct and the universe to guide you in the past, so if it tells you to let go, then listen!

5) You know you will only heal once the process is complete. Sometimes the wounds you have endured are too deep and any further communications will only cause pain, and you aren't willing to take that path.

## What to Take Away from a Twin Flame Relationship

First, realize that this relationship is unlike any other. You may have ended it and gone your separate ways, but you will still be part of your twin no matter what. When you part, it is normal to go through the traditional feelings of grief, anger, and hatred, followed by acceptance and forgiveness. Embrace all these emotions and use them to assimilate the lessons you have learned.

You need to celebrate the good times and let go of the bad experiences. This is the way your soul develops and steps closer to your spiritual transformation. Your twin flame relationship will stay with you, and while it may have ended in this reality, you will meet again!

# Chapter 9: Stage 6: The Surrendering

This stage of the twin flame journey has been described as the magic formula or silver bullet of the process. You need to give up the final vestiges of power you have over your destiny. You reach a point when you understand that being powerless is possibly the most powerful way to live. The key is to realize what you have and let go of the attachment you may have to things and people you may think you need, but you know you can't have.

You need to believe that the universe has your destiny covered. You need to lose the fear that the relationship with your twin is based on your ego and actions. Surrender yourself to the divine and let go of the residual parts of the experience you still feel you control. Imagine your union as a rose. You have been happy to give the petals to the universe, yet you have hung on to the thorns. You are unwilling to let go of your partnership's shadowy areas, and you still cling to the sore points and moral challenges because your ego is telling you they are shameful.

Surrendering is all about realizing that you don't get to choose what parts of your love you show to the world. This depiction of your relationship needs to be whole before you can understand how it works. Roses wouldn't exist with just petals; the thorns need to be included as essential parts of the whole flower.

You need to open your mind and body to the love you have with your twin flame and let it ascend earthly boundaries. Your ego is a lust-filled part of you that seeks judgment and thrives on the boundaries society puts in place. But why should you be held back by such material boundaries? The whole point of a twin flame relationship is to transcend the barriers that exist when it comes to love. You need to accept that your love will not be restricted or imprisoned by differences and conformities. You will allow yourself to love unconditionally no matter what the obstacles in place.

### A Higher Love

Surrendering to your flame means you are walking away from society's paradigms and becoming part of a more spiritual way of loving. So, what if your twin flame is from a different culture or religion to you? Are they in a relationship with someone else? Guess what? Relationships end all the time. If they want to be with you, it will happen. Parents that stay together for the sake of children is an old-fashioned concept that rarely works out well. Surrendering is all about putting yourself first and allowing your needs to be met. Every time you put yourself last, you are putting everybody else last as well.

Are you ready to be brave and refuse to waste another lifetime ruled by fear? Break away from traditional ties and face the world with a confident belief in yourself. Let yourself heed the call of the exquisite yet illogical form of love because it is meant to be. No matter what the barriers society places before you break them down and live the life ruled by destiny. The universe won't give up on you, and it will follow you until you become emancipated and embrace your twin flame experience with every fiber of your being.

# What to Expect When You Surrender

When your ego governs you, you believe that inner peace is only possible when the world is aligned, and everything is perfect. When you surrender, you embrace the notion that only when you feel at peace will everything fall into place. So basically, you are turning your world upside down and changing your belief system.

You will also learn of the many realizations that will help you accept your fate.

**1) You Will Focus Less on Your Twin Flame Relationship and Begin to Focus on Yourself.**

**2) The Connection You Have with Your Twin Will be Filled with Happiness:** You now know that every negative emotion you project will radiate back and cause you harm because you are a mirror image of each other.

**3) The Only Part of Your Twin Flame Connection You are in Control of is Your Own:** You can't control how they think or react.

**4) In the Past, You Have Been Drawn to Emotionally Harmful Relationships, and You Felt They Were Your Destiny:** That is why you were constantly looking for flaws in the union with your twin flame.

**5) You Will Lose the Need for More Fulfillment:** You become appreciative of what you have and become grateful for every moment.

**6) You Will Be More Comfortable Alone:** You don't need other people to complete you because you are filled with positive energy.

**7) Communication with Your Twin Flame Will Be More Vivid:** Once you accept that the universe is responsible for your fate as a couple, then you will use other means to be together. Use the astral plane to spend time with your partner and talk to them. Share a cuddle or just lie together in harmony. These connections will be just as real as physical interactions.

**8) You Will Find Yourself Sending Love to Your Twin Regularly:** Telling them you love them will encourage them to respond when they feel ready.

**9) You Will Slow Down:** Modern life is hectic, and it can become overwhelming. When you surrender to your destiny, it takes the pressure off you to keep up with the rest of society. Symptoms of this pressure include headaches, nausea, and breathing issues, so when you slow down and take your time, you will feel healthier and more grounded.

**10) You Will Become Interested in Your Shared Synchronicities:** Instead of being annoyed by the bonds that connect you, your shared interests and feelings will reassure you that, no matter what happens, this person will be in your life forever. You will become more aware that the things that are happening to you are probably happening to them as well. Send telepathic messages when you feel this connection and ask them to respond.

**11) You Will Become More Interested in the Bond Between Science and Spirituality:** Once you stop obsessing about what is going to happen in the future, you free up your mind to explore different subjects. If you were previously attracted to science subjects at school, you might seek knowledge from the spiritual world. Books about spirituality will appeal to you. Crystals and amulets will become part of your world while you feel the need to visit important spiritual places. Your next vacation may be somewhere as diverse as a retreat or a trip to India to visit a guru. If you are naturally spiritual, then the world of science will become appealing. Try subscribing to Science News, a bi-weekly publication that brings news from recent science and technical journals. The articles are short, professionally written, and packed with fascinating information written in layman's terms.

**12) You Will be More Aware of the Changes in Your Twin's Tempo and How to Deal with Them:** In the past, you may have felt these differences in mood and energy levels were a disruptive part of your relationship, but now you know better. You aren't meant to be completely in tune with each other because when you have different issues, you need to come together as a unit and deal with them. Even though you are separated, you still need to work in this way. Your telepathic connection doesn't mean they have constant access to your thoughts.

Here are simple ways you can improve your telepathic skills:

- **Start with Simple Messages and See How Clear They are When Your Partner Receives Them**: Send a color or shape to begin with, and then add another element.

- **Lose Fear:** Just like surrendering to the twin flame relationship, it's time to let go of negativity. Society may not believe in telepathy as a relevant way of communicating, but you already know it is. As twin flames, you have been communicating with each other for many lifetimes. Believe in your skill and accept that the more you practice, the better at it you will become.

- **Use Props to Improve the Strength of Your Signal:** Crystals, candles, and other aids help you concentrate and focus on your mission. Turn a room in your house into a spiritual place and use it to send your telepathic messages. You shouldn't limit your messages to your twin flame. Talk to the universe and tell it your thoughts; it will listen and respond.

- **Power Up the Thought with Positivity:** When you send your thoughts, bathe them in a clear white light before you let them go. Feel the energy buzzing in your mind and send it to your chosen recipient.

- **Visualize Communication:** As you send your message, imagine how it will be received. Will your twin be joyful at your communication? Sometimes when you are apart, visualization will help you feel more connected.

There are codes and ethics connected to telepathy that shouldn't be ignored. Just as you value your privacy, so does your twin. Create a telepathic shield or cloak when you want to keep your thoughts secret. This should be something that both of you should do openly. You need to have mutual respect and be comfortable with your conversations on all planes.

**13) You Will Experience Total Love:** Once you let go of fear and doubt, you create the space for even more love. You recognize how your ego has distorted how you look at them, but now you have a clearer picture. This non-judgmental state of mind will let you recognize the depth of your love. They are amazing! They are the most amazing person in the universe. Your heart will swell with love and devotion for them even if you never meet them again.

**14) When You Look into Their Eyes, You Will See a Representation of Your "Original" Environment:** This is the origin of your soul. This is the place where you feel most comfortable. It can happen when you look into their eyes face to face, or it can happen even when separated. A picture of them may seem normal to other people, but it shines with energy to you. As you look into the eyes, you see a deep space lit with the divine light that fills your soul with hope. To you, your twin is like an angel in the darkness, always there to guide you and fill your soul with love.

**15) You Will Feel a Purely Physical Pull:** Once the spiritual connections are perfected, then the natural way to progress is on the physical plane. If the universe believes the time is right, it will put you on the right path to reconciliation. As with other situations, now is the time to follow the signs it sends you. If you suddenly receive an invitation to visit a new area, then accept it. If you see a deal on a trip that seems too good to be true, grab the opportunity, and it could lead you to your twin.

The universe is a minx when it comes to communicating with you! It can cause you to be affected by a sign simply designed to let you know it is there. A sense of physical touch could be a sign from the universe you are loved. If you feel a warm touch on your shoulder when you feel down, it is your divine self-giving you a positive sign. If you suddenly get goosebumps without the temperature changing, this means someone somewhere is having intense, passionate thoughts about you. A white feather or butterfly is also a classic sign you are communicating with the astral plane.

**16) You Will Reach a Startling Conclusion About Your Relationship:** You will both become accepting that your relationship with each other is the last and most complete union you will ever have. But what if this relationship doesn't survive your separation and fails to reach the reunion stage? That's okay as well. You have been part of the most intense and magical couplings imaginable.

Even if you are relatively young in human terms, your soul is not subject to the same aging process. If your soul is mature enough to accept that the relationship will survive no matter what the physical world throws at it, then it will be okay with the outcome. If your soul is relatively new to the spiritual realm, then it may experience some bruising. Don't worry; this is all part of your spiritual being's aging process, and you will emerge stronger and ready for your next union in another life.

**17) You Will Discover a New Life Plan:** Once you surrender to the process of twin flame unions, you will drop any false teachings that have governed your life previously. You will still be interested in environmental issues and feel an affinity to the planet, but you will know your place. Your life mission shouldn't be dedicated to healing any rifts in society or repairing any damage to the earth. Your mission should be about you, your love, and your connection with your twin. You are no longer interested in wasting time online envying other people. The world of celebrities and all the baggage they bring will be so irrelevant you wonder why it ever had any interest in the past. You will discover a thirst for knowledge that leads you to study more worthy subjects dear to your heart.

**18) You Won't Care What Society Thinks Anymore:** Your natural sense of style will emerge. You fail to conform and are more willing to flex your quirky personality. Your clothes may become more "out there," and you experiment more with your look.

**19) You Will Embrace Your Inner Child:** What did you love to do as a child? Do you still do it, or have you abandoned it as a childish pursuit. Maybe you loved to paint or draw as a child, but you don't have the time anymore. Make time. Instead of chilling out with Netflix, try hanging out with a sketchpad. Use your imagination to create works of art that reflect your personality. Surrendering is all about letting your natural instincts free.

Buy yourself skates or a skateboard and try out some moves at a local park. Who cares if you fall off and people laugh at you? You don't! Forget man-made teachings and how you appear to others. You have the perfect union with yourself when you form a connection with your flame, so all other opinions are muted. Did you ever regret something you didn't do? Then now is the time to do it. You have all the free time in the world once you let the universe take over your destiny, so use it to grow spiritually and physically.

**20) You Will Relearn How to Experience Things:** Next time you see a sporting event or an essential cultural experience on TV, consider what is happening. Are the people concentrated on what is happening, or can you just see a blanket of smartphones trying to picture the event? Modern society is so focused on recording events and experiences they have forgotten how to enjoy the natural joy and energy surrounding them. Leave your device at home and go out and experience the world. You don't care anymore what your online profile looks like, so why should you feel the need to photograph everything? Don't let technology interfere with your psyche. Let go of it and become a participant in life rather than a spectator.

When you surrender to your destiny, then you feel reborn. It is the highest form of acceptance and you recognize that any blocks you have in life are *your responsibility*. You will stop assigning blame to your twin, and when you do so, you will feel a purer form of love for them. When you make these personal shifts, you may find the obstacles that keep you apart from your twin disappear. The universe will determine if you are blessed with a reunion, and it will work tirelessly to get you together with them if that is your fate.

# Chapter 10: Stage 7: Twin Flame Reunion or Joining

The end of the journey is in sight. The happily ever after a phase when you will both become one and the world will accept you as a couple. The separation will have been different for every couple. Your twin could have moved away and cut off all contact, or they may still live in the same house as you, but they have distanced themselves emotionally.

Maybe you and your partner have been stuck on the revolving wheel of separation and reunion for some time. You may have experienced exhausting cycles of drama and fear, followed by love and passion. This can happen when the two partners are at varying stages of spiritual growth. Unfortunately, some couples fail to reach the reunion stage as they are stuck in the 3D world and have failed to ascend. If this happens to you, don't worry; you have multiple lives ahead of you to reconnect with your twin flame.

The main thing to remember is this final union is unique for everyone and can follow varying periods of separation. Some people may have been apart for years as they both had issues that needed to be dealt with. Life is often complicated for twin flames as one or both halves of the couple may have emotional baggage that keeps them from committing.

Fortunately, some commonalities signal a reunion is about to happen. If you have experienced a feeling that your twin is using a "dangling carrot" type of thinking about your situation, then you may feel it's time to resolve your relationship. You will know when it is time to act and overcome your doubts and misgivings. This may cause a union between the two of you, or it may not. Whatever the outcome, when the signs occur, you must act on them. What happens next is determined by destiny and will give you peace of mind.

## Signs That a Reunion is About to Happen

**1) Excitement:** Are you feeling butterflies in your stomach for no reason at all? Do you wake up with a feeling of joy and anticipation? This may be a sign from your heart chakra that something amazing is about to happen. Your soul is incredibly intuitive when it comes to your twin flame, and it will sense if a shift in their feelings has happened. You may have already surrendered to your union, but they may have held back. Internal excitement can signal they are now ready to reunite.

**2) Communication Between the Two of You is More Harmonious:** You may have had periods when all communications ceased or became fractious. You may have lost contact completely. If you suddenly find messages from them on social media or they appear in your dreams, then this is a sign they want to reconnect. Both of you may have moved since you last saw each other and are unaware of how to get in touch physically, but that won't stop you. Twin flames may be thousands of miles apart, but they will always be close on the astral plane.

**3) Your Twin Flame Commitments May Have Changed:** As a spiritual being, people in twin flame relationships have a common belief that their connection shouldn't interfere with another soul's contract on Earth. If your twin was already committed to someone else, then this may be part of the reason you separated. If you hear that their situation has changed, this may be a sign they will return to you. While this may be the perfect outcome for the two of you, be aware that other people will be hurt during the process. Spiritual wounds may be deeper than earthly ones, but the pain of separation is still considerable. But if you are currently putting your life on hold as you sit in a cosmic waiting room contemplating your twin and their partner breaking up, then you need to leave! Your twin has the free will needed to leave earthly relationships, and it is their choice to stay. You couldn't and shouldn't interfere. Get on with the rest of your life and find new opportunities for love.

**4) The Reflection Principle:** If thoughts of your twin have receded during your separation, you may be surprised to find yourself thinking about them a lot recently. This is a sign that something has shifted in your relationship, and you may be ready to reconcile. The term reflection principle means that if your thought patterns have changed, then so have your twins. Be aware that your counterpart feels the increase in intensity of feelings just as strongly as you do.

You may even find that their name crops up every time you converse with other people. If your friends and family have asked you how your twin is or if you have heard from them, take note! This is a sure sign from the universe they are destined to come back into your life. The spiritual plane is preparing you and your immediate circle of acquaintances for their reappearance. Watch out for old photos and memories that include your twin on social media. Facebook memories are especially attuned to your spiritual vibrations and can surprise you with a jolt from the past.

**5) They Will Appear While You Meditate:** If you have experienced signs that your twin is ready to reunite, but you aren't sure if this is true or merely wishful thinking, then try meditation for more concrete answers. This powerful tool is especially effective when you have questions that can't be answered by more traditional methods. Write down the purpose of your meditation on a piece of paper before you start the process. Now begin your chosen method of meditation and focus your thoughts on your twin flame. Ask if they are ready to become part of your union again. Are they going to be getting in touch soon, or are you misreading the signs? Sometimes you will feel like the answers you seek are beyond you, and even meditation is proving fruitless. Don't worry; the reasons you aren't getting answers may be beyond your control. There could be obstacles in place within yourself or your twin delaying the process. You are always given guidance, but you may have limiting barriers inside your psyche.

**6) An Irresistible Draw to Places and Events:** Do you feel like the universe is nudging you to get out more? This is a common sign that something is about to happen. We have discussed in other chapters how these signs may manifest. Sometimes you may be overwhelmed with conflicting signs hard to follow, or there may be a lack of input that makes you feel abandoned and alone. Take heart in the fact that the universe is a constant companion and is forever sending you information. When you are on a dark road and feeling like your future is uncertain, then you need only one light to guide you home. The dark road of your twin flame journey has been a rocky one, but the end is in sight.

The universe can lead you to a secondhand bookstore where you find a reference to a long-forgotten coffee shop you once used. When you revisit the coffee shop, you just happen to bump into a friend who knows your flame. You meet later in the week, and your twin reappears in your life.

You could even be involved in a minor car crash with a man who works with your twin flame. All coincidences will lead to your twin and a reunion. There are coincidences and blessings in disguise sent by the universe to nudge you in the right direction, so even the worst experiences can lead to positive outcomes.

**7) Inner Peace:** When you experience the surrendering phase, you automatically change your thought process. You understand that most things are out of your control, and that's okay. When you surrender, it is part of the process of awaiting reunion; however, paradoxically, when you give up on any chance of reunion, this can be the most potent sign of all. Once you find that all thoughts of a reunion and a happy life together have left you, you are in a state of inner wholeness. This radiates into outer wholeness, and when you realize that you need nobody else to complete you, or your life is the most likely time you will reunite.

**8) You Feel Like They are with You Already:** Have you felt like your twin is sitting right next to you? Has it reached the point where you turn toward them and starting a conversation even though you know they are miles away? When all barriers are down, and you are both spiritually ready for a reunion, then you will experience it on an astral plane first. Your divine timings are attuned, and the universe is preparing you both. You may even feel the need to adjust your home to be ready for your union. You will know instinctively if they are coming to you or if you need to move. You may find yourself looking at real estate in certain areas or checking out job vacancies in other areas. You will feel the spirit of your twin sharing their thoughts with you when you least expect it, and you will be comforted by their spiritual presence.

**9) You Will Become More Creative:** If you find yourself contemplating writing a novel for the first time or find yourself reading poetry, then a recoupling with your twin may be in the cards. Your soul may typically be more interested in practicalities and keeping your life ordered and organized, but you also feel energized as you feel more excited. Your creative juices will start flowing as you become more entwined with nature and beauty. You know the world is an amazing place to be, and you will feel an overwhelming desire to capture its beauty artistically. These pieces of creativity will give you something to share with your twin as you reunite. You are about to enter your union's highest expression, and you want to surround yourself with positive images and literature.

**10) Recognize How Numbers Can be Used to Send Messages:** Spiritual messages can take various forms, but one of the most powerful can be numbers. This could be because, during a regular day, we are inundated with numerical influences.

Consider these examples:

- When you pay a bill online, what do you need? A customer number, a card number, a final sum of how much to pay, and maybe a time of delivery are all necessary. These aspects are numerical.

- When traveling, what is the most important thing you need to check? Time, of course. What time is your train leaving, how long will the journey take, and what time is your connection?

- Shopping: Everything you buy has a monetary value. Every receipt will contain a multitude of numbers.

- Going to the Gym: If you think you can avoid numbers when getting fit, think again! You will have a certain number of reps to do and different exercises are designed to last for a specific length of time.

- Chill Out: Even at our most relaxed time is an important part of our routine. What time is your favorite program on? How many hours can you spend playing Xbox?

With this in mind, is it any wonder that the universe uses the power of numbers to influence us and remind us they are in control. Understanding what the numbers mean is an art that needs to be learned.

## How to Recognize What Numbers are Trying to Tell You

Some people call the spiritual use of numbers numerology, while others call the process angel numbers. The reasoning behind sequences and their meanings are based on the geometric plan of the universe. While the spiritual guides that govern your life are constantly communicating with you, they know that the spiritual journey you are on is particularly important. Your twin will be receiving similar levels of guidance and will also be subject to numerical influences.

## Master Numbers

The first of the master numbers is 11, the second is 22, and the third is 33. They represent the intuition and insight connected to your subconscious and gut feelings. Within the twin flame experience, they can play a major part in influencing you to ready yourself for a meeting or reunion between the two of you. Chances are, you will have witnessed the appearance of the first master number, 11, as you entered the yearning phase. Still, as you prepare yourself for a reunion, you will find it playing a special role in your life once again.

The perfect angel number is 1111, and it acts as a spiritual wake-up call to get ready for momentous events. So, if you are shopping in a store and your receipt is a sequence of 1's, then this tells you that you are currently part of the energy of the earth. Your cleansed spirit is at the perfect point to reach the zenith of your relationship. If the sequence is interspersed with the number 5, this can also be significant and indicate that positive times lie ahead. The number 8 signifies that a positive opportunity is in the cards for you.

Platonic relationships between twin flames can also gain guidance from numerology. The master number 11 can be combined with the number 7 to indicate a strong union that isn't based on sex or attraction. The sequence 7117 or 717 can be causally related to the tarot card that depicts the Lover. But, as tarot readers will tell you, this doesn't necessarily mean a sexual union. The numbers 6 and 9 will also make an appearance if you need a nudge to change your focus. 6 is an indication that you may be focusing too much on negative aspects, while 9 suggested that you are too focused on the material parts of your life. Both numbers indicate you should return to more spiritual pursuits.

The master number 22 is sent by your guides to encourage you to be more confident. Often referred to as the *master-builder*, it is used to encourage you to turn dreams into reality. It is meant to fill you with hope for the future and a confident outlook for your relationship.

With your relationship's reunion stage, you will be sent connections containing the master number 33. It is often called the master teacher and is more powerful because it is a combination of 11 and 22, which elevates it to the top level. The number 33 has no personal message to send. Instead, it is a sign that all humanity is about to experience a higher level of emotion. For those people waiting for signs of a possible reunion, it is a sign you have achieved a higher spiritual plane. Signs of the number 33 combined with recurring 11's are the most significant signs from your guide that your reunion is imminent.

# What Happens Once You Have Rejoined Your Twin?

Once the separation phase has ended and you have both surrendered to your union, then the reunion will happen. You can't force it or screw it up; it just happens when you are both ready for this connection. You know you are meant to be together, and your subconscious minds will begin to merge, and you will be aware of each other's individual explicit awareness.

**You Understand Three Things**

    **1) The Significance of Your Partnership:** You know each other so well that you are comfortable with your separate roles within the relationship. You may be a typical male/female couple who believe that your sex governs your roles. The woman will become responsible for the relationship's mental health and will take charge of the communication between you. The male partner will take on the role of protector and be responsible for the home and feeding the family. Less conventional couples will feel comfortable enough to assign roles without gender influences. The important thing to remember is that you are comfortable with your relationship and you can be honest with one another.

    **2) When You Work Together, You Form an Unbeatable Team:** In the past, you will have had conflicts with the power you have in the union. You separated for a reason, and one of the main reasons could be you resisted working together. Now you have reunited, you are confident in your individual strengths, and you know that you are peerless when you combine your efforts.

**3) You are Meant to Live Together:** In the past, you may have struggled to live under the same roof because you need your personal space. Now you could live in a cupboard and be happy! You have recognized that being together anywhere makes that place the best place in the world. You will no longer argue over where you will live; you will decide together.

# Conclusion

Are you ready to meet your twin flame? Does the thought of such an intense experience appeal to you, or are you still hesitant? This book was written to help you regardless of the stage you are in. Hopefully, it has helped you realize who is in your life for a specific reason and who will be there for you, always. Life is all about the relationships you form. Good luck in making the right choices, and remember, keep looking for signs from the universe!

# Here's another book by Mari Silva that you might like

# References

A Little Spark of Joy - Everything Tarot and life's Higher Vibes. (n.d.). Retrieved from https://www.alittlesparkofjoy.com/

ASK ANGELS For Help With Any Request! Contact Your Angels. (n.d.). Askingangels.com.

containhe01. (n.d.). Containhe01. Retrieved from https://www.newagedream.com/

CosmicMinds.com is for sale. (n.d.). HugeDomains. Retrieved from https://www.hugedomains.com/domain_profile.cfm?d=cosmicminds&e=com

Elite Daily. (n.d.). Elite Daily. https://www.elitedaily.com/

Forever Conscious. (n.d.). Forever Conscious. http://www.foreverconscious.com

Hack Spirit. (n.d.). Hack Spirit. Retrieved from https://hackspirit.com/

Home. (n.d.). HipLatina. Retrieved from https://hiplatina.com/

Home - Awake and Align | Beyond Quantum Healing Hypnosis. (n.d.). Awake and Align. Retrieved from https://awakeandalign.com/

My Twin Soul Journal. (n.d.). My Twin Soul Journal. Retrieved from https://mytwinsouljournal.blog/

Nast, C. (n.d.). Allure - Beauty Tips, Trends & Product Reviews. Allure. Retrieved from http://www.allure.com

PowerofPositivity. (n.d.). Power of Positivity: #1 Positive Thinking & Self Help Community. Power of Positivity: Positive Thinking & Attitude. Retrieved from https://www.powerofpositivity.com/

Simply the best online psychic readings available anywhere - Psychic Elements. (n.d.). Psychicelements.com. Retrieved from https://psychicelements.com/

Supernatural Vibrations Home. (n.d.). Supernatural Vibrations. Retrieved from https://www.supernaturalvibrations.com/

The Mother Loving Future- Consciousness + Parenting. (n.d.). The Mother Loving Future. Retrieved from http://www.themotherlovingfuture.com/

Torgerson, R. (2019). Cosmopolitan.com - The Women's Magazine for Fashion, Sex Advice, Dating Tips, and Celebrity News. Cosmopolitan; Cosmopolitan. http://www.cosmopolitan.com

Twin Flamez – Zero's & One's with some added Two's. (n.d.). Retrieved from https://www.twinflamez.com/

Walk the path less traveled ★ LonerWolf. (n.d.). LonerWolf. Retrieved from http://www.lonerwolf.com

(2021). Orchidrecovery.com.

Printed in Great Britain
by Amazon